The European Sovereign Debt Crisis and Its Impacts on Financial Markets

T0360913

The global financial crisis saw many Eurozone countries bearing excessive public debt. This led the government bond yields of some peripheral countries to rise sharply, resulting in the outbreak of the European sovereign debt crisis. The debt crisis is characterized by its immediate spread from Greece, the country of origin, to its neighbouring countries and the connection between the Eurozone banking sector and the public sector debt. Addressing these interesting features, this book sheds light on the impacts of the crisis on various financial markets in Europe.

This book is among the first to conduct a thorough empirical analysis of the European sovereign debt crisis. It analyses, using advanced econometric methodologies, why the crisis escalated so prominently, having significant impacts on a wide range of financial markets, and was not just limited to government bond markets.

The book also allows one to understand the consequences and the overall impact of such a debt crisis, enabling investors and policymakers to formulate diversification strategies and create suitable regulatory frameworks.

Go Tamakoshi is a Research Fellow at Department of Economics of Kobe University in Japan. He received his PhD in Economics from Kobe University, MBA from MIT Sloan School of Management, MS and MPP from the University of Michigan, Ann Arbor, and BA from Kyoto University. He has published many papers in refereed journals, such as *European Journal of Finance, Applied Financial Economics*, and *North American Journal of Economics and Finance*.

Shigeyuki Hamori is a Professor of Economics at Kobe University in Japan. He received his PhD from Duke University and has published many papers in refereed journals. He is the author or co-author of *Rural Labor Migration, Discrimination, and the New Dual Labor Market in China* (Springer, 2014) and *Indian Economy: Empirical Analysis on Monetary and Financial Issues in India* (World Scientific, 2014). He is also the co-editor of *Global Linkages and Economic Rebalancing in East Asia* (World Scientific, 2013) and *Financial Globalization and Regionalism in East Asia* (Routledge, 2014).

The European Sovereign Debt Crisis and Its Impacts on Financial Markets

Go Tamakoshi and Shigeyuki Hamori

Routledge
Taylor & Francis Group

LONDON AND NEW YORK

First published 2015
by Routledge
2 Park Square, Milton Park, Abingdon, Oxon OX14 4RN

and by Routledge
711 Third Avenue, New York, NY 10017

First issued in paperback 2017

Routledge is an imprint of the Taylor & Francis Group, an informa business

British Library Cataloguing in Publication Data
A catalogue record for this book is available from the British Library

Library of Congress Cataloging-in-Publication Data
Tamakoshi, Go.
   The European sovereign debt crisis and its impacts on financial markets / Go Tamakoshi and Shigeyuki Hamori.
      pages cm
   1. Debts, Public—Europe.   2. Capital market—Europe.
3. Economic development—Econometric models.   I. Hamori, Shigeyuki, 1959–   II. Title.
   HJ8015.T36 2015
   332'.0415094—dc23
   2014029393

ISBN 13: 978-0-8153-5074-3 (pbk)
ISBN 13: 978-1-138-79907-3 (hbk)

Typeset in Times New Roman
by Apex CoVantage, LLC

Contents

List of figures   xi
List of tables   xiii
About the authors   xv

Introduction   1

PART I
How were dynamic correlations among financial markets
changed by the crisis?   9

1 Co-movements among stock markets of European
**   financial institutions**   11

  1.1 Introduction 11
  1.2 Empirical methodology 13
  1.3 Data 14
  1.4 Empirical results 17
  1.5 Conclusion 22
     References 23

2 Co-movements among GIIPS national stock indices   25

  2.1 Introduction 25
  2.2 Empirical methodology 27
  2.3 Data 28
  2.4 Empirical results 29
  2.5 Conclusion 34
     References 35

3 Co-movements among European exchange rates   37

  3.1 Introduction 37
  3.2 Empirical methodology 39
  3.3 Data 41

3.4 Empirical results 42
3.5 Conclusion 48
    References 50

PART II
How were causalities among financial markets
altered by the crisis?   53

4 The causality between Greek sovereign bond yields
   and southern European banking sector equity returns   55

4.1 Introduction 55
4.2 Empirical methodology 57
4.3 Data 59
4.4 Empirical results 60
4.5 Conclusion 68
    References 69

5 Causality between the US dollar and the euro
   LIBOR-OIS spreads   71

5.1 Introduction 71
5.2 Data 73
5.3 Empirical results 74
5.4 Conclusion 79
    References 80

6 Causality between the Euro and Greek sovereign CDS spreads   82

6.1 Introduction 82
6.2 Empirical methodology 84
6.3 Data 85
6.4 Empirical results 87
6.5 Conclusion 91
    References 92

PART III
When did structural changes in financial markets
occur due to the crisis?   95

7 Structural breaks in the volatility of the Greek
   sovereign bond index   97

7.1 Introduction 97
7.2 Data 98

7.3 Empirical results 99
7.4 Conclusion 105
   References 106

**8 Structural breaks in spillovers among banking
   stock indices in the EMU**   108

8.1 Introduction 108
8.2 Empirical methodology 110
8.3 Data 111
8.4 Empirical results 113
8.5 Conclusion 119
   References 120

**9 Structural breaks in the relationship between the Eonia
   and Euribor rates**   121

9.1 Introduction 121
9.2 Empirical methodology 122
9.3 Data 123
9.4 Empirical results 124
9.5 Conclusion 128
   References 128

First publication of each chapter   131
Index   133

Figures

1.1	Daily DCCs for each pair of the five financial institutions	19
2.1	Estimated dynamic equicorrelation under the DECO model	31
3.1	Rolling correlations between each foreign currency pair	44
3.2	Dynamic conditional correlations between each foreign currency pair	45
4.1	Causality-in-mean and causality-in-variance by Q-tests from lag 1 up to lag M (M = 5, 10, or 15)	67
5.1	3-month LIBOR-OIS spreads in US dollars (USD) and euro (EUR) (in percentage)	73
6.1	Movement of the Greek CDS spreads and the NEER for the euro	85
6.2	Generalized impulse responses to a one-standard deviation shock (pre-crisis period)	89
6.3	Generalized impulse responses to a one-standard deviation shock (crisis period)	90
7.1	Returns of the 10-year Greek government bond index (percentage), April 1999–March 2012	103
7.2	Conditional variances of the 10-year Greek government bond index, April 1999–March 2012	103
8.1	Total return spillover plot – estimated using 200-week rolling windows (in percentage)	114
8.2	Total volatility spillover plot – estimated using 200-week rolling windows (in percentage)	115
8.3	Net return spillovers – estimated using 200-week rolling windows (in percentage)	117
8.4	Net volatility spillovers – estimated using 200-week rolling windows (in percentage)	118
9.1	Historical paths of the Eonia rate (EON) and the 3-month Euribor rate (ER3)	123
9.2	Response of the Eonia rate (EON) and the 3-month Euribor rate (ER3) to error correlation	126
9.3	Timing of the 'extreme' regime (Regime 2) derived from threshold VECM estimation (shaded area)	127

Tables

1.1	Summary of statistics on the stock returns	15
1.2	AR-GARCH model estimation	18
1.3	Principal components analysis of stock returns	19
1.4	Dynamic conditional correlation estimates of the stock returns	19
1.5	AR(1) models for the estimated DCC coefficients	21
2.1	Summary statistics of stock index returns	28
2.2	Estimation of the AR-EGARCH model and the DECO model	30
2.3	Dynamic equicorrelation and crisis periods	32
2.4	Dynamic equicorrelation and economic factors	33
3.1	Basic statistics on exchange rate returns	41
3.2	Empirical results of univariate AR-GARCH models	42
3.3	Principal components analysis of exchange rate returns	43
3.4	Dynamic conditional correlation (DCC) estimates of exchange rate returns	44
3.5	Estimation of AR models for the estimated DCC coefficients: sensitivity analysis	46
4.1	Summary of statistics	61
4.2	Results of ADF unit root tests	62
4.3	Results of AR-EGARCH models	63
4.4	Cross correlation analysis between Greek bond yields and Greek banking stock indices	65
4.5	Cross correlation analysis between Greek bond yields and Portuguese banking stock indices	66
4.6	Cross correlation analysis between Greek bond yields and Italian banking stock indices	66
4.7	Cross correlation analysis between Greek bond yields and Spanish banking stock indices	67
5.1	Summary of statistics	74
5.2	Unit root tests: ADF	74
5.3	Results of AR-EGARCH models	75
5.4	Hong (2001) cross-correlation analysis	78
6.1	Summary of statistics	86
6.2	Results of ADF unit root tests	87

xiv *Tables*

6.3	Results of Granger causality tests in LA-VAR framework	88
7.1	Basic statistics for returns of the 10-year Greek government bond index	99
7.2	Model estimation: AR-EGARCH versus AR-GARCH	100
7.3	Empirical results of the Bai and Perron (1998, 2003) tests	102
7.4	Model estimation: AR–EGARCH with dummies in mean and variance	104
8.1	Summary statistics of the EMU banking stock index return	112
8.2	Summary statistics of the EMU banking stock index volatility	112
8.3	Spillover table of the EMU banking stock index return	113
8.4	Spillover table of the EMU banking stock index volatility	114
9.1	Unit root tests	124
9.2	Tests for threshold cointegration between the Eonia rate and the 3-month Euribor rate	124
9.3	Threshold VECM estimation between the Eonia rate and the 3-month Euribor rate	125

About the authors

Go Tamakoshi is a Research Fellow at Department of Economics of Kobe University in Japan. He received his PhD in Economics from Kobe University, MBA from MIT Sloan School of Management, MS and MPP from University of Michigan, Ann Arbor, and BA from Kyoto University. He has published many papers in refereed journals, such as *European Journal of Finance*, *Applied Financial Economics*, and *North American Journal of Economics and Finance*.

Shigeyuki Hamori is a Professor of Economics at Kobe University in Japan. He received his PhD from Duke University and has published many papers in refereed journals. He is the author or co-author of *An Empirical Investigation of Stock Markets: the CCF Approach* (Kluwer Academic Publishers, 2003), *Hidden Markov Models: Applications to Financial Economics* (Springer, 2004), *Empirical Techniques in Finance* (Springer, 2005), *Introduction of the Euro and the Monetary Policy of the European Central Bank* (World Scientific, 2009), *Rural Labor Migration, Discrimination, and the New Dual Labor Market in China* (Springer, 2014), and *Indian Economy: Empirical Analysis on Monetary and Financial Issues in India* (World Scientific, 2014). He is also the co-editor of *Global Linkages and Economic Rebalancing in East Asia* (World Scientific, 2013) and *Financial Globalization and Regionalism in East Asia* (Routledge, 2014).

Introduction

The global financial crisis, which began in the US subprime loan market in 2007, heavily affected the banking industry across the world. It culminated with the bankruptcy of Lehman Brothers on 15 September 2008. The Eurozone banking system was not segregated from such developments. Indeed, governments in the Euro area rescued the financial institutions that were considered systematically important. As a result, some peripheral economies, countries usually known as GIIPS (Greece, Ireland, Italy, Portugal, and Spain), bore an excessive burden of public debt. The government bond yields of these nations rose sharply, with a perceived deterioration of their creditworthiness. Greece became the first country to lose investor confidence in its capacity to repay the debt, which resulted in the onset of the European sovereign debt crisis. The nation agreed on a bailout package with the EU and the International Monetary Fund (IMF) in May 2010, followed by Ireland in November 2010 and Portugal in May 2011. Nonetheless, the bailouts did not attenuate the crisis throughout 2011 and 2012, with the sovereign risks of Spain and Italy to be the next under scrutiny by market participants. Observing this background, economists usually regard the debt crisis as a by-product of the global financial crisis (e.g. Arghyrou and Kontonikas, 2012; Kalbaska and Gatkowski, 2012; Ahmad et al., 2013).

Some aspects of the institutional framework of the European Monetary Union (EMU) also may have made member countries more vulnerable to increases in their sovereign default risks. Introducing the single currency implied that each country could no longer rely on monetary policies in order to pursue devaluation in improving its price competitiveness or to facilitate inflation for reducing the real value of its debt (Klose and Weigert, 2014). In addition, abandoning national currencies led to the member countries depending more on fiscal policies as countercyclical macroeconomic measures, potentially resulting in increases in their budget deficits (Gali and Monacelli, 2008; Lane, 2012). To address these potential issues, an initial design of the EMU included such requirements as the Stability and Growth Pact (SGP) that set limits on the percentage of budget deficits and the ratio of public debt to GDP, as well as the 'no-bailout' clause of the Maastricht Treaty that prohibited a member country from assuming the debts of another country. However, such formal rules turned out to be insufficient in depressing the incentives to incur excessive debts, which were inherent in the institutional features of the EMU in the case of national governments of some peripheral countries (Baltatescu, 2013; Whelan, 2013).

This book is motivated by the following three intriguing aspects of the recent European sovereign debt crisis. First, the crisis originated in the government bond market of a relatively developed nation such as Greece, although high sovereign debt risks had historically been associated with emerging countries. Specifically, until the inception of the recent financial turmoil, it had been widely believed that government bonds of Eurozone countries, including Greece, would bear no country-specific risks, as euro-denominated bond markets were extremely standardized. This belief was supported by the so-called 'convergence trade' hypothesis, contending that investors' purchases of the bonds of peripheral European nations were justified by the scenario in which their yields would achieve a full convergence to that of Germany (Oliveria et al., 2012). In fact, since the introduction of the euro until mid-2007, the spreads of long-term government bond yields of almost all other Eurozone countries with that of German bond yields had narrowed substantially. Hence, under the 'convergence trade' hypothesis prevailing in markets, Eurozone countries felt little pressure to utilise public finances effectively. Therefore, it is interesting to see that the recent debt crisis occurred in a place where little attention was paid to the possibility of sovereign default.

Second, the debt crisis immediately spread from Greece, a country contributing only a small fraction of the Eurozone's total GDP, to Ireland and Portugal and further affected even Italy and Spain to a lesser extent. Such a spillover manifested in the form of sharp increases in sovereign bond spreads between these peripheral countries of the EMU and Germany. GIIPS countries had experienced the deterioration of fiscal and other macroeconomic fundamentals for the period 2001–2009, and then, after the onset of the debt crisis, sovereign bond markets began to place heavier penalties on such macroeconomic imbalances (Arghyrou and Tsoukalas, 2011; Arghyrou and Kontonikas, 2012). Interestingly, recent empirical studies have found evidence that sudden increases in sovereign bond spreads can be viewed as a 'wake-up call' contagion. It is a phenomenon where a crisis, initially restricted to one country, supplies new information which triggers investors' reassessment of the default risk of other nations and, thereby, the crisis is spread to other countries (Mink and Haan, 2013; Giordano et al., 2013).

Third, the debt crisis is characterised by the connection between the Eurozone banking sector and public sector debt. A deteriorated banking sector can cause a contraction of the economy because of the limited credit flow available. This potentially exacerbates the fiscal outlook through the decline in present values of future tax streams. The risk transfer from the banking to the public sector can occur if governments intervene to bail out troubled banks (Gray et al., 2008; Acharya et al., 2011; Alter and Schuler, 2012). Such linkages between banking and sovereign risks are complicated by the fact that Eurozone banks hold substantial amounts of sovereign debt. The dramatic increases in the sovereign bond yields of GIIPS countries implied that the banking sector in the area would suffer from the impairment of their balance sheets (Arnold, 2012; Bruyckere et al., 2013). It is worthwhile to note that before the debt crisis, this subtle relationship between the banking sector and the public sector had not attracted much attention from the policymakers in the EMU.

The main objective of this book is to shed light on the impacts of the European sovereign debt crisis on various financial markets in Europe. Particular attention is paid to the impacts of the crisis on dynamic correlations among financial markets (Part I); the impacts of the crisis on causalities among financial markets (Part II); and the timing of structural changes in financial markets due to the crisis (Part III). As the analysis presented in this book uncovers, the crisis not only affected the sovereign bond markets of vulnerable GIIPS countries but also altered the inter- and intra-country relationships of other financial markets across the entire Eurozone. Indeed, the three unique and interesting features of the debt crisis presented earlier help us to understand why the crisis escalated so prominently, having significant impacts on a wide range of financial markets. Moreover, this book also contributes to drawing implications for investors and policymakers who wish to use the knowledge of the consequences of the recent debt crisis. We now provide a brief overview of each chapter.

Part I: How were dynamic correlations among financial markets changed by the crisis?

Chapter 1 is titled 'Co-movements among stock markets of European financial institutions'. This chapter investigates the dynamic relationships between the stock returns of five important financial institutions in the Eurozone, whose exposure to Greek government bonds was particularly high. We use the multivariate dynamic conditional correlation (DCC) model of Engle (2002) and then assess the impacts of the global financial crisis and the European debt crisis, employing autoregressive models with crisis dummy variables. Despite differences in core businesses and location of headquarters, we find significant increases in the dynamic correlations for some pairs of financial institutions during the global financial crisis. In addition, contrary to the results of previous studies such as Savva (2011), we also detect significantly positive effects of the sovereign debt crisis on the DCC estimates for several pairs, indicating the existence of contagion effects. These findings imply the diminished benefits of diversification for global traders by holding stocks of financial institutions across various countries during the recent financial turmoil. We also argue that regulators should pay attention to the exposure of European financial institutions to the deteriorated sovereign risk of Greek government bonds and the resulting systemic risks, as reflected in the increased DCC estimates between their stock returns.

Chapter 2 is titled 'Co-movements among GIIPS national stock indices'. This chapter examines the dynamic interrelationships among the national stock index returns of Greece, Ireland, Portugal, Italy, and Spain. We employ the dynamic equicorrelation (DECO) model of Engle and Kelly (2012) and assess potential driving factors, such as the recent financial turmoil in Europe and several other economic variables, for the evolution of the estimated dynamic equicorrelation, with autoregressive models. We detect substantial fluctuations of the estimated equicorrelation over time and, specifically, significant increases in the co-movements during both the global financial crisis and the European sovereign debt crisis periods. Further, we find that the global risk aversion factor, represented by the US corporate–government bond spread, also increased the equicorrelation significantly. Our findings suggest that for traders, portfolio diversification effects among the national stock indices were rather limited when they were most needed, namely during the two crises that hit Europe. Our empirical results also highlight the need for policymakers to recognize that contagion in the equity markets can occur even in a debt crisis, which originated in sovereign bond markets, and to conduct policy coordination in order to avoid contagion among the affected countries.

Chapter 3 is titled 'Co-movements among European exchange rates'. This chapter analyses the time-varying linkages of three US dollar (USD) exchange rates expressed in the euro (EUR), British pound (GBP), and the Swiss franc (CHF). We adopt the multivariate, asymmetric DCC model of Cappiello et al. (2006) and conduct a sensitivity analysis for impacts of the recent European crises on the dynamic correlations by employing autoregressive models with crisis dummies. We detect asymmetric responses in the correlation between the three exchange rate returns, namely, higher dependency during periods of joint appreciation than during periods of joint depreciation. We also find significant decreases in the estimated DCCs for the CHF–EUR pair, particularly after the debt crisis, and for the GBP–CHF pair, especially after the global credit crisis. These findings imply that global investors may identify more diversification opportunities, owing to the lower degree of dependency between the exchange rates, during crisis periods. In addition, the high level of interdependence during the pre-crisis period may indicate the difficulty faced by policymakers in controlling exchange rates only through local monetary policies. Moreover, our findings of the dynamic dependence between the exchange rates will help policymakers to decide whether and how they need to implement foreign exchange market interventions.

Part II: How were causalities among financial markets altered by the crisis?

Chapter 4 is titled 'The causality between Greek sovereign bond yields and southern European banking sector equity returns'. This chapter investigates cross-country mean and volatility transmission effects between Greek long-term bond yields and the banking sector stock returns of four southern European countries (Greece, Portugal, Italy, and Spain), with a focus on uncovering impacts of the European sovereign debt crisis. We use the cross-correlation function approach of Hong (2001). We find that the causality-in-mean effects vary across countries, casting a doubt on the assumption of a unidirectional causality, from interest rates to stock returns, which is commonly used in economic literature. More importantly, we detect evidence of bidirectional causality-in-variance effects between Greek long-term bond yields and the banking sector equities of Portugal, Italy, and Spain, which emerged after the onset of the debt crisis. Our findings on the complex linkage between the public sector debt and the banking sector are of great importance for both bank managers and regulators in the region. In particular, the empirical results may suggest the need to monitor volatility spillovers between government bonds of one country, faced with increasing sovereign risks, and the banking sector stocks of a neighbouring country, in order to prevent cross-country contagion effects.

Chapter 5 is titled 'Causality between the US dollar and the euro LIBOR-OIS spreads'. This chapter empirically analyses causality-in-mean and causality-in-variance between the USD and EUR LIBOR-OIS spreads, which are viewed as measures of liquidity stress and credit risk, in the interbank markets. We apply the cross-correlation function approach of Hong (2001) to examine the lead-lag relationships of mean and volatility transmissions. During the global financial crisis, we find not only significant bidirectional mean transmissions between the two spreads, consistent with the results of previous studies, but also significant unidirectional volatility transmissions from the EUR to the USD spread. The identified difference underscores the importance of policymakers to monitor causality-in-variance between the spreads, as it can capture information flow in the interbank markets and thus represent potential root causes of apparent instability. Moreover, we detect no significant causality at the mean and variance levels between the spreads during the debt crisis period. This provides support for the view that several of the measures that the European Central Bank (ECB) took to boost liquidity in the wake of the debt crisis were effective at least in terms of eliminating contagion effects in the interbank markets, as reflected in the no-causality observed between the LIBOR-OIS spreads.

Chapter 6 is titled 'Causality between the Euro and Greek sovereign CDS spreads'. This chapter examines the causal relationships between the value of the EUR and the Greek sovereign credit default swap (CDS) spreads, with the 3-month EUR LIBOR as a control variable. We employ the lag-augmented VAR (LA-VAR) methodology of Toda and Yamamoto (1995) to test for long-run Granger-causality between the series and then adopt the generalized impulse response function (G-IRF) analysis of Koop et al. (1996) and Pesaran and Shin (1998) to assess short-run effects in responses to shocks. We find evidence of significant causality from the EUR to the Greek sovereign CDS spreads during the debt crisis period, which is reinforced by the G-IRF analysis. Throughout the sample period, no significant causality from the Greek CDS spreads to the EUR is identified, while the EUR LIBOR significantly Granger-causes the EUR. Our findings imply that policymakers should be aware of potential transmission effects from variability in the exchange rate to the sovereign CDSs in times of market turbulence. It is also suggested that from the traders' perspectives, the Greek sovereign CDS spreads are a less valuable indicator than the EUR LIBOR for predicting EUR exchange rate movements.

Part III: When did structural changes in financial markets occur due to the crisis?

Chapter 7 is titled 'Structural breaks in the volatility of the Greek sovereign bond index'. This chapter investigates the presence of structural changes in the mean and volatility of the 10-year Greek sovereign bond index returns. The multiple structural break test of Bai and Perron (1998, 2003) is employed. We find that there exists one break date in both mean and volatility, April 2010, when the European sovereign debt crisis intensified and the Greek long-term bond was downgraded to junk status. After incorporating the identified break date into our mean and variance equations, we derive superior estimation results. A positively significant coefficient of the dummy variable of the structural break in variance indicates a regime shift triggered by the debt crisis. In addition, our measure of volatility persistence decreases sharply after the dummy variables are included. The empirical results are useful for traders, in that incorporating the structural change may enable them to improve their forecasts of volatility of the sovereign bond and, thereby, their performance in portfolio risk management. Furthermore, our findings on the timing of the volatility regime shift may help policymakers to identify potential causes for the bond market's turbulence and, hence, implement regulatory measures to prevent their adverse effects.

Chapter 8 is titled 'Structural breaks in spillovers among banking stock indices in the EMU'. This chapter analyses time-varying return and volatility spillovers among banking sector stock indices in seven Eurozone countries (GIIPS, Germany, and France), and explores the presence of structural breaks. We use the spillover index of Diebold and Yilmaz (2012). We find that on average, a large portion of forecast error variance comes from cross-country spillovers of returns and volatilities. The volatility spillover plot is less stable than that of the return spillover, and exhibits bursts that coincide with events representing the global credit crisis, implying the occurrence of regime shifts. However, it declines sharply after early 2009, perhaps due to the several monetary policies implemented by the ECB to improve liquidity conditions during the debt crisis. We also uncover that Italy and Spain are net transmitters of both return and volatility spillovers, whilst Greece, Ireland, and Portugal are net receivers. The identified patterns of time-varying returns and volatility spillovers are useful for investors pursuing portfolio diversification and timely risk management. Furthermore, policymakers can use the spillover measures used in this chapter to monitor and prevent contagion effects from the banking sector stock indices in other countries.

Chapter 9 is titled 'Structural breaks in the relationship between the Eonia and Euribor rates'. This chapter examines the linkage between two important short-term interests, the Eonia rate and the 3-month Euribor rate, and analyses potential regime shifts in their dynamic relationship. We use the threshold vector error correction model (VECM) approach of Hansen and Seo (2002). We reject the null hypothesis of linear cointegration between the interest rates and thus find that the two-regime threshold cointegration model is more appropriate. We show that in a 'typical' regime, error correction occurs only through the adjustment of the Eonia rate, which can be viewed as the operational target of the ECB. This is not consistent with the conventional view of the expectations hypothesis. The short-run response is driven by the Euribor rate only in an 'extreme' regime, which corresponds to the period of the global financial crisis and the period of the intensified European sovereign debt crisis (especially in December 2011). Our findings on such asymmetric behaviours of the two key interest rates are of great relevance to European policymakers in terms of predicting potential impacts of monetary policies and assessing the efficacy of affecting the very short-term interest rates in the interbank money market.

Acknowledgement

The authors are grateful to Ms. Yongling Lam for excellent editorial work. This research in part supported by a Grant-in-Aid of the Japan Society for the Promotion of Science.

References

Acharya, V., Drechsler, I., Schnabl, P. (2011) A Pyrrhic victory? Bank bailouts and sovereign credit risk, NBER Working Paper no. 17136, National Bureau of Economic Research, Cambridge, MA.

Ahmad, W., Sehgal, S., Bhanumurthy, N.R. (2013) Eurozone crisis and BRIICKS stock markets: Contagion or market interdependence? *Economic Modelling*, **33**, 209–225.

Alter, A., Schüler, Y.S. (2012) Credit spread interdependencies of European states and banks during the financial crisis, *Journal of Banking & Finance*, **36**, 3444–3468.

Arghyrou, M.G., Kontonikas, A. (2012) The EMU sovereign-debt crisis: Fundamentals, expectations and contagion, *Journal of International Financial Markets, Institutions & Money*, **22**, 658–677.

Arghyrou, M.G., Tsoukalas, J.D. (2011) The Greek debt crisis: Likely causes, mechanics and outcomes, *The World Economy*, **34**, 173–191.

Arnold, I.J.M. (2012) Sovereign debt exposures and banking risks in the current EU financial crisis, *Journal of Policy Modeling*, **34**, 906–920.

Bai, J., Perron, P. (1998) Estimating and testing linear models with multiple structural changes, *Econometrica*, **66**, 47–78.

Bai, J., Perron, P. (2003) Computation and analysis of multiple structural change models, *Journal of Applied Econometrics*, **18**, 1–22.

Baltatescu, I. (2013) Eurozone public debt problem: An analysis from the perspective of the institutions and policies, *Global Economic Observer*, **1**, 83–92.

Bruyckere, V.D., Gerhardt, M., Schepens, G., Vennet, R.V. (2013) Bank/sovereign risk spillovers in the European debt crisis, *Journal of Banking & Finance*, **37**, 4793–4809.

Cappiello, L., Engle, R., Sheppard, K. (2006) Asymmetric dynamics in the correlations of global equity and bond returns, *Journal of Financial Econometrics*, **4**, 557–572.

Diebold, F.X., Yilmaz, K. (2012) Better to give than to receive: Predictive directional measurement of volatility spillovers, *International Journal of Forecasting*, **28**, 57–66.

Engle, R. (2002) Dynamic conditional correlation: A simple class of multivariate generalized autoregressive conditional heteroskedasticity models, *Journal of Business and Economic Statistics*, **20**, 339–350.

Engle, R., Kelly, B. (2012) Dynamic equicorrelation, *Journal of Business & Economic Statistics*, **30**, 212–228.

Galí, J., Monacelli, T. (2008) Optimal monetary and fiscal policy in a currency union, *Journal of International Economics*, **76**, 116–132.

Giordano, R., Pericoli, M., Tommasino, P. (2013) Pure or wake-up-call contagion? Another look at the EMU sovereign debt crisis, *International Finance*, **16**, 131–160.

Gray, D. F., Merton, R. C., Bodie, Z. (2008) New framework for measuring and managing macrofinancial risk and financial stability, NBER Working Paper No. 13607, National Bureau of Economic Research, Cambridge, MA.

Hansen, B.E., Seo, B. (2002) Testing for two-regime threshold cointegration in vector error-correction models, *Journal of Econometrics*, **110**, 293–318.

Hong, Y. (2001) A test for volatility spillover with application to exchange rates, *Journal of Econometrics*, **103**, 183–224.

Kalbaska, A., Gatkowski, M. (2012) Eurozone sovereign contagion: Evidence from the CDS market (2005–2010), *Journal of Economic Behavior & Organization*, **83**, 657–673.

Klose, J., Weigert, B. (2014) Sovereign yield spreads during the euro crisis: Fundamental factors versus redenomination risk, *International Finance*, **17**, 25–50.

Koop, G., Pesaran, M. H., Potter, S. M. (1996) Impulse response analysis in nonlinear multivariate models, *Journal of Econometrics*, **74**, 119–147.

Lane, P.R. (2012) The European sovereign debt crisis, *Journal of Economic Perspectives*, **26**, 49–68.

Mink, M., Haan, J. (2013) Contagion during the Greek sovereign debt crisis, *Journal of International Money and Finance*, **34**, 102–113.

Oliveria, L., Curto, J.D., Nunes, J.P. (2012) The determinants of sovereign credit spread changes in the Euro-zone, *Journal of International Financial Markets, Institutions & Money*, **22**, 278–304.

Pesaran, M.H., Shin, Y. (1998) Generalized impulse response analysis in linear multivariate models, *Economic Letters*, **58**, 17–29.

Toda, H.Y., Yamamoto, T. (1995) Statistical inference in vector autoregressions with possibly near integrated processes, *Journal of Econometrics*, **66**, 225–250.

Whelan, K. (2013) Sovereign default and the euro, *Oxford Review of Economic Policy*, **29**, 478–501.

Part I

How were dynamic correlations among financial markets changed by the crisis?

1 Co-movements among stock markets of European financial institutions

1.1. Introduction

The recent European sovereign debt crisis, which originated from the downgrade of Greek government bonds in late 2009, points to the necessity of understanding how shocks in one financial market spread to other markets. In May 2010, policymakers in the European Monetary Union (EMU) agreed on a bailout package for Greece and to establish a 440 billion euro European Financial Stability Facility (EFSF). Following Greece, Ireland and Portugal faced a serious deterioration in their public finances and requested assistance from the EFSF, the former in November 2010 and the latter in April 2011. It appears the debt crisis is still plaguing the region, with Spain and Italy now also facing increases in government bond spreads.

The debt crisis manifests in soaring government bond spreads within the affected nations. Economics literature has investigated the potential causes of the European debt crisis and has proposed two main hypotheses. First, the bond spread increases seem to be driven by country-specific fiscal imbalances and macroeconomic fundamentals. These include the current account deficit and business cycle, as indicated by some recent empirical studies (e.g. Arghyrou and Kontonikas, 2012; Oliveira et al., 2012). The second hypothesis, as proposed by Archarya et al. (2011), reflects the importance of the linkage between the banking sector and the public sector. A troubled banking sector may trigger an economic recession by limiting the credit flow to the private sector, which leads to a fiscal imbalance. In turn, the increase in sovereign credit risks may burden the banking sector because public debt is largely held by European banks.

The present study sheds light on the interrelationship between the banking sector and public debt, a topic to which little attention has been paid by the empirical literature. In July 2011, the European Banking Authority released the results of its stress tests on important European banks. The findings caused serious concern among European policymakers with regard to the solvency of Greece, as many large European financial institutions have a significant Greek government bond exposure. The tests showed that the main private sector financial institutions have an aggregate net exposure of 83 billion euro to Greek sovereign debts. As a result, a 21% write-off on those debts could trigger losses of approximately 17 billion euro across the 90 banks studied.

Based on these results, we investigate the time-varying correlations of stocks between major European financial institutions to determine whether there is evidence of contagion, with particular emphasis on the sovereign debt crisis period. Here, we study five financial institutions, selected primarily based on the amount each holds in Greek government bonds, according to a recent report by Barclays Capital[1]. The first institution included in the study is the National Bank of Greece (NBG), the largest holder (13.2 billion euro) among the Greek commercial banks. The remaining four banks are the top four holders among non-Greek European financial institutions: BNP Paribas (BNP), Dexia (DEX), Generali (GEN), and Commerzbank (COM). These institutions hold 5.0 billion, 3.5 billion, 3.0 billion, and 2.0 billion euro of Greek government bonds, respectively. Each of these financial conglomerates, which operate across Europe, has its headquarters in a different country, as well as a slightly different core business. Therefore, studying the correlations among the movement of the stocks of these institutions may provide interesting insights. The National Bank of Greece is the largest commercial banking group, with a strong ATM network in Greece and a strong presence in south-eastern Europe. BNP Paribas, headquartered in Paris, is an investment banking group with interests not only in Europe, but also in the US and Asia. Dexia, a Belgian financial institution, primarily provides retail banking services and asset management. Generali, headquartered in Trieste, Italy, is the second largest insurance conglomerate in Europe, by revenue, after AXA. Commerzbank, headquartered in Frankfurt, Germany, has strengths in commercial banking and mortgaging but is now expanding into investment banking. Each institution was affected by the global financial crisis that originated from the US subprime loan markets in February 2007, but each has survived the financial turmoil thus far.

Economists have used various definitions for 'contagion'. However, a number of recent studies assessing the impacts of financial crises seem to have reached the consensus that contagion refers to a significant increase in the correlation across financial markets that exists only when extreme shocks are triggered during turbulent periods (e.g. Forbes and Rigobon, 2002). In this context, the DCC approach suggested by Engle (2002) is one of the main econometric tools used to identify time-varying correlations of asset prices across nations. The DCC framework and its various modified versions have been used extensively to assess the impacts of financial crises (e.g. Yang, 2005; Chiang et al., 2007; and Kuper and Lestano, 2007, for the Asian financial crisis, and Cheung et al., 2008; Yiu et al., 2010; and Liquanc ct al., 2010, for the global subprime loan crisis). The framework also has been used to analyse the impact of the introduction of the euro on the dynamics of correlations (e.g. Bartnum et al., 2007; Kenourgios et al., 2009; Savva et al., 2009). In terms of triggering systemic solvency risks across nations, these studies focused on the dynamic conditional correlations among national stock indices rather than the linkages between major financial institutions in the banking and insurance sectors.

The only study to specifically investigate interbank relations during financial crisis periods was conducted by Savva (2011). This study employed three versions of the DCC model to determine how the correlations among four multinational investment banking stocks evolved through the global financial crisis. The study used the original DCC model proposed by Engle (2002), the smooth transition conditional correlation model (STCC) of Berben and Jansen (2005), and the double STCC (DSTCC) model of Silvennoinen and Terasvirta (2009). The four banks studied were Goldman Sachs, the Royal Bank of Scotland, Societe Generale, and Deutsche Bank. The study found that the correlations between these banks increased at the beginning of the crisis but generally exhibited a sharp decline toward late 2008. The author concluded that the decreases in the correlations were consistent with the network theory of contagion suggested by Allen and Babus (2008), according to which the interconnectedness of banks that serve to ensure a smaller probability of systemic failure tends to deteriorate during financial turmoil. Due to Savva's sample period (3 January 2006 to 27 February 2009) and rather arbitrary choice of banks, this study did not analyse the impacts of the recent Greek sovereign debt crisis.

To the best of our knowledge, the present study is among the first to explicitly examine how the sovereign debt crisis has influenced the time-varying linkages of major European financial institutions. We empirically demonstrate that the correlations for some combinations of financial institutions (4 out of 10) increased sharply during the debt crisis, suggesting that contagion occurred across financial sectors in various EMU nations. The financial contagion during the crisis implies that the risk diversification for global traders across the stock prices of the main financial institutions may be diminished. It also suggests that regulators should pay close attention to the systemic risks in financial sector stocks with regard to their risk exposure to Greek bonds.

The remainder of the article is organized as follows. Section 1.2 briefly summarizes the econometric methodology. Section 1.3 offers a detailed description of our dataset. Section 1.4 provides our empirical results and Section 1.5 presents concluding remarks.

1.2.   Empirical methodology

In order to examine the dynamic conditional correlation, we take the following three steps. First, we estimate the conditional means and variances of each stock return using univariate autoregressive generalized autoregressive conditional heteroskedasticity (AR-GARCH)[2] models. Our approach differs from the similar study by Savva (2011) in that instead of simply assuming that each conditional mean and variance follow a GJR-GARCH(1,1) process, we select the best of the AR(k)-GARCH(p,q) models using a generalized error distribution (GED). Let us denote the return and the error term for stock j by $r_{j,t}$ and $\varepsilon_{j,t}$. Then, the conditional mean and variance of returns can be denoted by

$$r_{j,t} = \phi_0 + \sum_{k=1}^{10} \phi_k r_{j,t-k} + \varepsilon_{j,t} \tag{1}$$

$$h_{j,t} = \omega + \sum_{p=1}^{2} \alpha_p h_{j,t-p} + \sum_{q=1}^{2} \beta_q \varepsilon_{j,t-q}^2, \tag{2}$$

where $h_{j,t}$ is the conditional variance of the returns series, and k (=1, 2, ..., 10), p (=1, 2), and q (=1, 2) are selected using the Schwarz Bayesian information criterion (SBIC).

Second, having determined the conditional variance from equation (2), we derive the conditional correlation using the multivariate DCC model developed by Engle (2002). Let us denote the conditional variance-covariance matrix as

$$H_t = D_t R_t D_t, \tag{3}$$

where D_t is the diagonal matrix of the conditional standard deviations extracted from equation (2) with $\sqrt{h_{j,t}}$ on the ith diagonal, and R_t is the time-varying correlation matrix.

Then, the evolution of the scalar version of the DCC model is given by

$$Q_t = (1 - a_1 - b_1)\overline{Q} + a_1 e_{t-1} e'_{t-1} + b_1 Q_{t-1}, \tag{4}$$

where $\overline{Q}$ is the unconditional covariance matrix of the standardized residuals, $e_{j,t} = \varepsilon_{j,t} / \sqrt{h_{j,t}}$, and a_1 and b_1 are nonnegative scalar variables that satisfy $a_1 + b_1 < 1$. Equation (4) is referred to as a DCC(1,1) model. The proper dynamic conditional correlation structure can be calculated by

$$R_t = Q_t^{*-1} Q_t Q_t^{*-1}, \tag{5}$$

where Q_t^* is a diagonal matrix containing the square root of the diagonal entries of the covariance matrix, Q_t.

Third, similar to Yiu et al. (2010), we apply AR(1) models to capture the conditional correlations derived from the second step. Two dummy variables ($Crisis_{1t}$ and $Crisis_{2t}$) are included to represent the global subprime loan crisis period (they take the value 1 from 8 February 2007 to 4 November 2009, and 0 otherwise) and the sovereign debt crisis period (they take the value 1 from 5 November 2009 to 30 June 2011, and 0 otherwise), respectively. This allows us to test whether each of the crises significantly altered the dynamics of the estimated conditional correlations between the financial institutions in our study. That is,

$$\hat{DCC}_t = \delta_0 + \delta_1 \hat{DCC}_{t-1} + \xi_1 Crisis_{1t} + \xi_2 Crisis_{2t} + v_t. \tag{6}$$

1.3.   Data

Our data contain the daily returns of the stock prices (1,329 samples in total) from 4 January 2006 to 30 June 2011 for the National Bank of Greece (NBG),

BNP Paribas (BNP), Dexia (DEX), Generali (GEN), and Commerzbank (COM). All data were taken from the Thomson Reuters Datastream. A daily stock return is the difference between the logarithm of the stock prices, multiplied by 100 to be expressed as a percentage. Data points that were unavailable owing to holidays in each country were eliminated from the sample. All indices are denominated in euros. Following Chiang et al. (2007), who applied the DCC framework to Asian stock markets, we used the daily closing price data[3], which provide us with a sufficient number of samples to examine the recent phenomena of the Greek sovereign debt crisis.

Table 1.1 shows a summary of the descriptive statistics for our dataset. The sample is divided into three periods. Sample A, ranging from 4 January 2006 to 7 February 2007, represents a relatively calm period before the two crisis periods. Sample B, from 8 February 2007 to 4 November 2009, includes the global subprime loan crisis period. We define 8 February 2007 as the beginning of the subprime loan crisis. This is the date that HSBC holdings announced it would be charging for its bad debts and when investors began to realize the seriousness of the subprime loan problem. Sample C, from 5 November 2009 to 30 June 2011, covers the Greek sovereign debt crisis period. It was early November that the Greek government disclosed that its fiscal deficit would be twice the amount previously announced, triggering investors' concerns about the nation's solvency. Over the entire sample period, all five institutions faced a negative mean return, as expected. NBG experienced their highest standard deviation in Sample C, while the other financial institutions experienced their highest standard deviation in Sample B. Jarque–Bera tests reject normality for all five companies across the sub-sample periods (except in the case of BNP in Sample A). According to the Augmented Dickey–Fuller (ADF) tests, there are no identifiable unit root processes for the stock return data at the 1% significance level.

Table 1.1 Summary of statistics on the stock returns

	NBG	*BNP*	*DEX*	*GEN*	*COM*
Entire sample (4 January 2006–30 June 2011)					
Mean (percentage)	–0.15	–0.02	–0.17	–0.05	–0.16
Median (percentage)	0.00	0.00	–0.05	0.00	0.00
Maximum (percentage)	16.25	18.98	28.77	12.31	20.97
Minimum (percentage)	–17.66	–20.18	–35.17	–8.81	–27.46
SD (percentage)	3.51	2.87	3.66	1.75	3.62
Skewness	–0.02	0.25	–0.20	–0.01	–0.46
Kurtosis	6.52	13.04	19.51	7.27	13.35
Jarque–Bera	685.19***	5,597.55***	15,099.02***	1,010.45***	5,978.42***

(*Continued*)

Table 1.1 (Continued)

	NBG	BNP	DEX	GEN	COM
Sample A (4 January 2006–7 February 2007)					
Mean (percentage)	0.03	0.09	0.06	0.04	0.07
Median (percentage)	0.00	0.13	0.05	0.00	0.15
Maximum (percentage)	9.98	5.04	2.75	6.91	5.49
Minimum (percentage)	−15.73	−4.41	−3.90	−4.56	−8.77
SD (percentage)	2.20	1.38	1.08	1.27	1.80
Skewness	−1.30	0.04	−0.48	0.50	−0.40
Kurtosis	15.15	3.52	4.29	6.25	5.38
Jarque–Bera	1,763.65***	3.18	29.58***	131.89***	72.19***
Sample B (8 February 2007–4 November 2009)					
Mean (percentage)	−0.07	−0.08	−0.22	−0.10	−0.23
Median (percentage)	0.00	−0.12	−0.18	−0.05	−0.18
Maximum (percentage)	15.95	18.89	28.77	7.95	20.97
Minimum (percentage)	−17.66	−20.18	−35.17	−8.81	−27.46
SD (percentage)	3.66	3.54	4.73	1.90	4.66
Skewness	−0.16	0.13	−0.21	−0.28	−0.27
Kurtosis	6.50	9.82	13.77	5.85	8.99
Jarque–Bera	339.94***	1,279.10***	3,188.85***	232.40***	992.27***
Sample C (5 November 2009–30 June 2011)					
Mean (percentage)	−0.41	0.00	−0.23	−0.04	−0.22
Median (percentage)	−0.80	0.03	−0.31	0.07	−0.16
Maximum (percentage)	16.25	18.98	15.93	12.31	8.56
Minimum (percentage)	−13.98	−7.70	−8.96	−5.79	−21.05
SD (percentage)	3.95	2.35	2.64	1.77	2.35
Skewness	0.41	1.01	0.62	0.51	−1.62
Kurtosis	4.77	13.48	6.68	9.04	18.47
Jarque–Bera	62.82***	1,878.37***	248.80***	618.98***	4,122.43***

Notes: Statistics for the difference of the logarithm of the daily stock prices, multiplied by 100, are reported.

*** denotes statistical significance at the 1% level.

1.4. Empirical results

AR-GARCH specification

We first fit the best of the univariate AR(k)-GARCH(p,q) models to each series of the stock returns. As shown in Table 1.2, we selected AR(1)-GARCH(1,1) based on the SBIC. The variance equations of each model exhibit a good fit to the dataset, with all parameters significant at a 10% level, showing the adequacy of our GARCH(1,1) specification. Moreover, the p-values of the Ljung–Box statistics, $Q(20)$ and $Q^2(20)$, are much larger than 0.01 for all five firms, suggesting no autocorrelation up to order 20 for standardized residuals and standard residuals squared, respectively. Nonetheless, the parameters in the mean equations are nonsignificant, even at the 10% level. However, this is not a major concern because our analysis focuses on the dynamics of the correlations of stock returns and, thus, is concerned only with whether the variance equations fit well.

Multivariate DCC models

We then estimate the DCC models developed by Engle (2002). The results of the principal component analysis for the five stock return series are given in Table 1.3. The first and largest principal component captures 60% of the total variation, while the explanatory power of the principal components declines substantially after subtracting this component. Hence, it can be inferred that one common factor drives a substantial portion of the total variation for the stock return series, despite the different nationalities and core business areas among the five financial institutions.

The results of the DCC estimates are given in Table 1.4. The estimates of the standardized residuals (a_1) parameter and of innovations in the dynamics of the conditional correlation matrix (b_1) are statistically significant at the 1% level. We also find that the condition $a_1 + b_1 < 1$ is satisfied. Therefore, we conclude that our multivariate DCC model specification fits the data well and, hence, we can use the derived DCC series to obtain a reasonable inference of the dynamics of correlations in the five financial institutions.

Figure 1.1 gives the estimates of the time-varying conditional correlations between each pair of institutions. First, the time-varying conditional correlations are largely unstable over the sample period. Thus, assuming the correlations to be constant would mislead investors or policymakers when assessing the diversification opportunities among these financial institutions. Second, for some combinations, the conditional correlations seem to exhibit structural (upward) breaks during the crisis periods as compared to the relatively calm period (Sample A). Examples include the conditional correlations between the National Bank of Greece and BNP Paribas in the subprime loan crisis period (Sample B) and between Dexia and Generali in the recent sovereign debt crisis period (Sample C). This motivates us to assess the impacts of the crises on the estimated dynamic conditional correlations using two dummy variables, the first

Table 1.2 AR-GARCH model estimation

	NBG AR(1)-GARCH(1,1)		BNP AR(1)-GARCH(1,1)		DEX AR(1)-GARCH(1,1)		GEN AR(1)-GARCH(1,1)		COM AR(1)-GARCH(1,1)	
	Estimate	SE	Estimate	SE	Estimate	SE	Estimate	SE	Estimate	SE
Mean equation										
φ_0	0.0217	0.0484	0.0206	0.0523	-0.0004	0.0096	0.0044	0.0389	0.0053	0.0839
φ_1	0.0154	0.0246	0.0113	0.0285	0.0004	0.0114	-0.0034	0.0279	0.0449	0.0554
Variance equation										
ω	0.1121**	0.0510	0.0641*	0.0330	0.0669*	0.0376	0.0812**	0.0328	0.0668***	0.0524
α_1	0.1243***	0.0252	0.0880***	0.0240	0.1364***	0.0282	0.0861***	0.0252	0.0859**	0.0363
β_1	0.8747***	0.0241	0.9043***	0.0240	0.8626***	0.0306	0.8877***	0.0296	0.9116***	0.0368
GED param.	1.4089***	0.0778	1.4641***	0.0888	1.2506***	0.0698	1.3113***	0.0769	1.1725***	0.0667
$Q(20)$	26.4070		20.0820		18.9360		14.2310		15.5250	
p-value	0.1530		0.4530		0.5260		0.8190		0.7460	
$Q^2(20)$	10.3720		17.0060		17.8640		14.6060		14.5560	
p-value	0.9610		0.6530		0.5960		0.7980		0.8010	

Notes: $Q(20)$ and $Q^2(20)$ are the Ljung–Box statistics up to the 20th orders in standardized residuals and standardized residuals squared, respectively.

***, **, and * denote statistical significance at the 1%, 5%, and 10% levels, respectively.

Table 1.3 Principal components analysis of stock returns

Variable	Eigenvalue	Cumulative value	Proportion of variances	Cumulative proportion
First principal component	2.9803	2.9803	0.5961	0.5961
Second principal component	0.6899	3.6703	0.1380	0.7341
Third principal component	0.5152	4.1855	0.1030	0.8371
Fourth principal component	0.4624	4.6479	0.0925	0.9296
Fifth principal component	0.3521	5.0000	0.0704	1.0000

Table 1.4 Dynamic conditional correlation estimates of the stock returns

Coefficient	Estimate	SE	Coefficient	Estimate	SE
a_1	0.0285***	0.0037	b_1	0.8899***	0.0371
Log-likelihood	−13567.8				

*** denotes statistical significance at the 1% level.

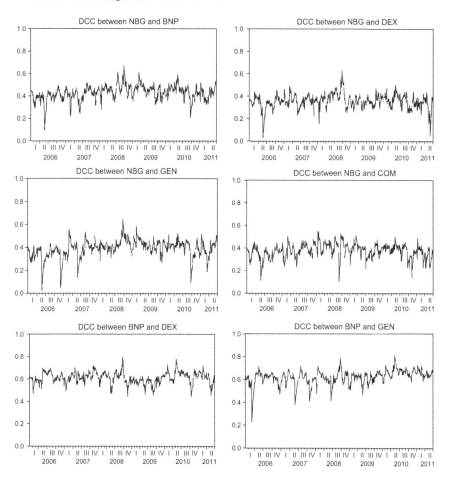

Figure 1.1 Daily DCCs for each pair of the five financial institutions

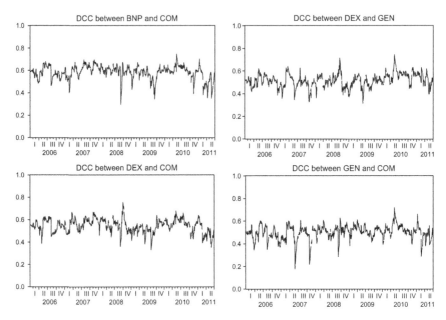

Figure 1.1 (Continued)

representing the US subprime loan crisis period and the second, the Greek sovereign debt crisis period.

AR model for the estimated DCC with dummy variables

We apply AR(1) models with the two dummy variables to the evolution of the estimated dynamic conditional correlations. Table 1.5 gives the estimation results of the regression models. The constant terms (δ_0) are all positive and significant at the 1% level. The coefficients of the AR terms (δ_1) are also significant for all cases at the 1% level with values of less than unity, showing a high level of persistence in the correlations. Moreover, high values of adjusted R^2 ensure the appropriateness of the AR(1) models.

The coefficients of the global subprime loan crisis dummies (ξ_1) are all positive and statistically significant at the 10% level for three combinations out of ten: between the National Bank of Greece and BNP Paribas, the National Bank of Greece and Generali, and the National Bank of Greece and Commerzbank. This is essentially in line with the findings of previous studies, such as that of Yiu et al. (2010), which documents a significant increase in the dynamic conditional correlations among several national equity indices during the subprime loan crisis. Furthermore, the coefficients of the sovereign debt crisis dummies (ξ_2) are also all positive and statistically significant at the 10% level for four combinations: between the National Bank of Greece and BNP Paribas, the National Bank of Greece and Generali, BNP Paribas and Generali, and Dexia and Generali. This

Table 1.5 AR(1) models for the estimated DCC coefficients

Estimated DCC between two financial institutions (respectively)

	NBG versus BNP		NBG versus DEX		NBG versus GEN		NBG versus COM		BNP versus DEX	
	Estimate	SE	Estimate	SE	Estimate	SE	Estimate	SE	Estimate	SE
δ_0	0.0299***	0.0044	0.0257***	0.0038	0.0275***	0.0040	0.0365***	0.0045	0.0400***	0.0061
δ_1	0.9230***	0.0106	0.9230***	0.0105	0.9152***	0.0110	0.8928***	0.0123	0.9340***	0.0098
ξ_1	0.0044**	0.0018	0.0027	0.0018	0.0077***	0.0022	0.0059***	0.0020	−0.0002	0.0013
ξ_2	0.0036*	0.0019	0.0011	0.0019	0.0062***	0.0022	0.0027	0.0021	0.0012	0.0014
Adjusted R^2	0.8671		0.8579		0.8708		0.8201		0.8759	

	BNP versus GEN		BNP versus COM		DEX versus GEN		DEX versus COM		GEN versus COM	
	Estimate	SE	Estimate	SE	Estimate	SE	Estimate	SE	Estimate	SE
δ_0	0.0452***	0.0044	0.0387***	0.0038	0.0348***	0.0040	0.0324***	0.0052	0.0390***	0.0054
δ_1	0.9245***	0.0106	0.9324***	0.0105	0.9306***	0.0110	0.9396***	0.0094	0.9184***	0.0109
ξ_1	0.0006	0.0018	0.0013	0.0018	0.0000	0.0022	0.0008	0.0015	0.0022	0.0018
ξ_2	0.0048***	0.0019	0.0000	0.0019	0.0034**	0.0022	0.0001	0.0016	0.0025	0.0019
Adjusted R^2	0.8808		0.8717		0.8836		0.8829		0.8479	

***, **, and * denote statistical significance at the 1%, 5%, and 10% levels, respectively.

implies that the debt crisis may have triggered regime shifts in correlations of the stock returns for these financial institutions, despite their differences in nationality and core business. These results contrast sharply with the findings of Savva (2011), who argued that the conditional correlations among four multinational investment banks dramatically declined toward the end of 2008, consistent with the network theory of contagion. Presumably, the observed significant increases in the estimated DCCs during the sovereign debt crisis period in our study can be attributed to contagion effects that intensified owing to the financial institutions holding substantial amounts of Greek government bonds.

Our results are relevant to international traders because precise correlation forecasting is critical to portfolio management decisions. The identified significant increases in the conditional correlations suggest that the benefits of international diversification by holding financial institution stocks across nations may have been reduced during the recent financial crises. Our findings are also useful to regulators. During the sovereign debt crisis in particular, it is likely that the substantial exposure of the main European financial institutions to Greek sovereign debts led them to face common systemic risks, as manifested in the increased degree of conditional correlations between their stock returns. These empirical results suggest that in order to prevent or cope with serious financial contagion across nations and financial sectors, regulators should be more aware of the exposure of financial institutions' stock prices in the EMU to the deteriorated credit risk of government bond markets in Greece, the origin of the debt crisis.

1.5.   Conclusion

Using the multivariate dynamic conditional correlation approach developed by Engle (2002), we investigated the time-varying relationships between the stock returns of five important European financial institutions. Our approach is unique in that we selected the institutions (the National Bank of Greece, BNP Paribas, Dexia, Generali, and Commerzbank) based on their exposure to Greek government bonds. We then modelled the estimated dynamic conditional correlations using autoregressive models with two crisis dummy variables, one representing the global financial crisis period and the other the recent European debt crisis period.

The key findings from our analysis are as follows. The conditional correlations are not constant over time and exhibit structural breaks during the recent financial crises, as compared to the pre-crisis period. Despite their differences in core business and location of headquarters, we detected significant increases in the DCC estimates for three out of ten pairs of the financial institutions studied during the global subprime loan crisis. Furthermore, the coefficients of the European sovereign debt crisis dummy are significant and positive for four out of ten pairs, suggesting the existence of contagion effects in the interbank relationships during the recent financial crises. This latter finding contrasts to those of Savva (2011). Overall, our results indicate the role of public sector debt and the banking sector during the recent European debt crisis and, hence, provide valuable insights to international traders and regulators in the EMU.

Notes

1 P. Ghezzi, A. Pascual, and F. Engles 'EURO THESIS Greece: what works and what does not', Barclays Capital, 11 July 2011. This analyst report lists the estimated top 40 holders of Greek government bonds and Greek debt.
2 Refer to Bollerslev (1986) for the GARCH model.
3 We recognize that using daily closing price data may underestimate the correlations between stock markets with non-synchronous trading hours. Nonetheless, using monthly or weekly data, we would be constrained by much smaller samples, which may be inefficient, especially using time-varying parameter approaches such as the DCC. See Martens and Poon (2001) for a more detailed discussion on the potential issues of using daily stock prices.

References

Allen, F., Babus, A. (2008) Networks in Finance, Wharton Financial Institutions Center Working Paper No. 08–07, Wharton Financial Institutions Center, Philadelphia, PA.

Archarya, V. V., Drechsler, I., Schnabl, P. (2011) A pyrrhic victory? Bank bailouts and sovereign credit risk, NBER Working Paper no. 17136, National Bureau of Economic Research, Cambridge, MA.

Arghyrou, M. G., Kontonikas, A. (2012) The EMU sovereign-debt crisis: Fundamentals, expectations and contagion, *Journal of International Financial Markets, Institutions and Money*, **22**, 658–677.

Bartnum, S., Taylor, S., Wang, Y. (2007) The Euro and European financial market integration, *Journal of Banking and Finance*, **31**, 1461–1481.

Berben, R. P., Jansen, W. J. (2005) Comovement in international equity markets: A sectoral view, *Journal of International Money and Finance*, **24**, 832–857.

Bollerslev, T. (1986) Generalized autoregressive conditional heteroskedasticity, *Journal of Econometrics*, **52**, 5–59.

Cheung, L., Fung, L., Tam, C. S. (2008) Measuring financial market interdependence and assessing possible contagion risk in the EMEAP region, Working Paper no. 18/2008, Hong Kong Monetary Authority, Hong Kong.

Chiang, T. C., Jeon, B. N., Li, H. (2007) Dynamic correlation analysis of financial contagion: Evidence from Asian markets, *Journal of International Money and Finance*, **26**, 1206–1228.

Engle, R. (2002) Dynamic conditional correlation: A simple class of multivariate generalized autoregressive conditional heteroskedasticity models, *Journal of Business and Economic Statistics*, **20**, 339–350.

Forbes, K., Rigobon, R. (2002) No contagion, only interdependence: Measuring stock market comovements, *Journal of Finance*, **57**, 2223–2261.

Kenourgios, D., Samitas, A., Paltalidis, N. (2009) Financial market dynamics in an enlarged European Union, *Journal of Economic Integration*, **24**, 197–221.

Kuper, G. H., Lestano, L. (2007) Dynamic conditional correlation analysis of financial market interdependence: An application to Thailand and Indonesia, *Journal of Asian Economics*, **18**, 670–684.

Liquane N., Naoui, K., Brahim, S. (2010) A dynamic conditional correlation analysis of financial contagion: The case of the subprime credit crisis, *International Journal of Economics and Finance*, **2**, 85–96.

Martens, M., Poon, S. (2001) Returns synchronization and daily correlation dynamics between international stock markets, *Journal of Banking and Finance*, **25**, 1805–1827.

Oliveira, L., Curto, J. D., Nunes, J. P. (2012) The determinants of sovereign credit spread changes in the Euro-zone, *Journal of International Financial Markets, Institutions and Money*, **22**, 278–304.

Savva, C. S. (2011) Modeling interbank relations during the international financial crisis, *Economics Bulletin*, **31**, 916–924.

Savva, C. S., Osborn, D. R., Gill, L. (2009) Spillovers and correlations between U.S. and major European stock markets: The role of the euro, *Applied Financial Economics*, **19**, 1595–1604.

Schwarz, G. (1978) Estimating the dimension of a model, *Annals of Statistics*, **6**, 461–464.

Silvennoinen, A., Teräsvirta, T. (2009) Modeling multivariate autoregressive conditional heteroskedasticity with double smooth transition conditional correlation GARCH model, *Journal of Financial Econometrics*, **7**, 373–411.

Yang, S. Y. (2005) A DCC analysis of international stock market correlations: The role of Japan on the Asian four tigers, *Applied Financial Economic Letters*, **1**, 89–93.

Yiu, M. S., Ho, W. A., Choi, D. F. (2010) Dynamic correlation analysis of financial contagion in Asian markets in global financial turmoil, *Applied Financial Economics*, **20**, 345–354.

2 Co-movements among GIIPS national stock indices

2.1. Introduction

This chapter investigates the time-varying interrelationships among the daily national stock index returns of Greece, Ireland, Italy, Portugal, and Spain (GIIPS hereafter) during the period January 2003 to December 2011. We use the dynamic equicorrelation (DECO) methodology by Engle and Kelly (2012) for this. The seminal work of Longin and Solnik (1995) contends that correlations among international stock markets fluctuate over time and tend to rise in bear markets. Our study is motivated by the importance of examining two main aspects of these time-varying stock market correlations across countries. First, changes in the correlations are of great importance to global investors, because these correlations are key inputs for cross-country portfolio allocation. Specifically, lower correlation across markets is a key to achieving global portfolio diversification and reducing portfolio risk without sacrificing returns (e.g. Grubel and Fadner, 1971). Second, changes in the cross-country linkage of stock returns are also crucial for policymakers. This is because an identified significant increase in stock market correlations is regarded as the presence of contagion (e.g. Forbes and Rigobon, 2002)[1], which may have great adverse effects on sustaining financial market stability. Thus, policymakers need to monitor the correlations closely in order to prevent cross-border contagion during market turbulence. Given this background, assessing the time-varying co-movement among GIIPS stock markets is worthy of scholarly attention. This is because in the wake of the recent financial turmoil, the national stock indices of these five most vulnerable countries in the EMU appeared to have experienced a series of coincidental and substantial drops.

Recently, studies on dynamic correlations among developed European stock markets have proliferated, spurred by the increased integration of these markets with the introduction of the euro. The following studies are some of the main examples of this. Kim et al. (2005) employed bivariate exponential general autoregressive conditional heteroskedasticity (EGARCH) models with time-varying correlations for the stock indices of 12 Eurozone and several non-Eurozone nations during 1989–2003. They found a regime shift in stock market integration after the introduction of the EMU. Bartram et al. (2007) used the time-varying copula approach for stock markets of 12 Eurozone and 5 non-European countries during 1994–2003. They showed that market dependence increased only for nations with large equity market capitalization and that the regime shift occurred in early 1998, when Eurozone membership was decided. Kearney and Poti (2006) applied the dynamic conditional correlation multivariate (DCC-MV) GARCH model to equity indices of the five largest Eurozone stock markets during 1993–2002 and identified the presence of a structural break in correlations at the beginning of monetary integration. They also found evidence of asymmetric responses of the correlations to positive and negative news.

Another line of research pays attention to the rapid transmission of shocks during the recent financial turmoil and its impact on European stock market correlations. For instance, Dajcman et al. (2012) used the DCC-GARCH model and wavelet correlation approach for the stock markets of Germany, France, Austria, and the UK during 1997–2010. They found that the correlations varied with time and were dependent on scale; furthermore, there was a slight, temporary increase in the already high level of correlations caused by the global financial crisis. Employing the asymmetric DCC (A-DCC) model and several copula models, Samitas and Tsakalos (2013) analysed the dynamic correlation between the Greek and seven European stock markets. Their findings indicated that although the US subprime loan crisis significantly increased the correlation, the Greek debt crisis had only a limited impact on the pairwise correlation of stock index returns between Greece and the seven other nations.

As compared to these studies, our analysis makes two primary contributions to the literature on the European stock market co-movement. First, we use the latest DECO framework by Engle and Kelly (2012) to investigate the correlation dynamics. The DCC approach, originally developed by Engle (2002), is often used to study the time-varying correlation of assets modelled along with volatilities. This approach enables us to reduce the computational complexity of traditional multivariate GARCH models, which involve estimating a large number of parameters. Nonetheless, the DCC model is considered cumbersome because it requires computation of $n(n-1)/2$ pairs of dynamic conditional correlations, which are difficult to interpret as the number of assets studied (n) grows. In contrast, the DECO model enables us to simplify the estimation by assuming that all pairwise correlations are still time-varying but are equal across assets at every time period. Furthermore, whereas the pairwise correlations in the DCC model depend only on the histories of two assets, the equicorrelation in the DECO approach can better assimilate the information by using the histories of all pairs of assets concerned.

Second, our study makes a detailed assessment of potential driving factors for the estimated dynamic equicorrelation derived from estimating the DECO model. By modelling the estimated equicorrelation with autoregressive models, we examine whether the European sovereign debt crisis and the global financial crisis had any significant impacts on the co-movement of GIIPS stock markets—specifically, whether the crises triggered a regime shift of the correlations. In addition, our regression analysis tries to identify whether several economic variables, such as exchange rate, interest rate, sovereign bond spread, and a factor representing the global risk aversion affected the GIIPS stock market correlation.

In sum, our empirical results reveal high variability of the estimated equicorrelation over time, with several peaks after 2007 in particular. In fact, we demonstrated evidence of contagion; that is, a significant increase in the dynamic equicorrelation among the GIIPS stock index returns during both the global financial and European debt crises. Further, we found that the US corporate–government bond spread, which signifies the global risk aversion of investors, significantly increased the GIIPS stock market co-movement, especially during the two crises.

The rest of the chapter is organized as follows. Section 2.2 briefly explains the econometric methodology—that is, the DECO model. Section 2.3 describes our data. Section 2.4 reports our empirical results and implications. Section 2.5 provides concluding remarks.

2.2.   Empirical methodology

Similar to a DCC model, the DECO model developed by Engle and Kelly (2012) can be estimated as follows. We first specify a return equation and a variance equation for each of the stock index returns by the univariate AR(1)-EGARCH(1,1) model[2] with a generalized error distribution (GED) as follows:

$$r_{i,t} = \phi_0 + \phi_1 r_{i,t-1} + \varepsilon_{i,t}, \tag{1}$$

$$\log(\sigma_{i,t}^2) = \omega + (\alpha_1 |z_{i,t-1}| + \gamma_1 z_{i,t-1}) + \beta_1 \log(\sigma_{i,t-1}^2), \tag{2}$$

where the standardized residuals $z_{i,t} = \varepsilon_{i,t}/\sigma_{i,t}$ are assumed to have a normal distribution with zero mean and unit variance.

We then estimate the dynamic equicorrelations, which the DECO model assumes to be equal across all the variables concerned at a given time. In this framework, the conditional variance–covariance matrix is denoted by

$$H_t = D_t R_t D_t, \tag{3}$$

where D_t is the diagonal matrix of the conditional standard deviations obtained by (2) with $\sigma_{i,t}$ on the ith diagonal. Here, R_t is an equicorrelation matrix with the dynamic equicorrelation ρ_t, which can be written as follows:

$$R_t = (1 - \rho_t)I_n + \rho_t J_n, \tag{4}$$

$$\rho_t = \frac{2}{n(n-1)} \sum_{i>j} \frac{q_{i,j,t}}{\sqrt{q_{i,i,t} q_{j,j,t}}}, \tag{5}$$

where I_n is an n-dimensional identity matrix, J_n denotes the $n \times n$ matrix of ones, and $q_{i,j,t}$ is the i, jth element of Q_t, the time-varying covariance matrix of the standardized residuals. Note that ρ_t above is computed as the average of the $n(n-1)/2$ correlations at time t. According to Engle and Kelly (2012), the scalar version of the DECO model specifies the evolution of Q_t as

$$Q_t = (1 - a - b)\overline{Q} + az_{t-1}z'_{t-1} + bQ_{t-1}, \tag{6}$$

where $\overline{Q}$ is the unconditional covariance matrix of the standardized residuals. By maximizing a log-likelihood function[3], we estimate the two parameters described in (6) above, namely, a and b. It is worthwhile to mention that in the DECO model, each bivariate combination of series (say, assets l and m among n number of assets) has the same correlation at a given time. Further, the dynamic equicorrelation depends on the histories of all pair of n assets, not those of assets l and m alone.

2.3.   Data

We use the daily Morgan Stanley Capital International (MSCI) stock index returns for Greece (GR), Ireland (IR), Portugal (PT), Italy (IT), and Spain (ES). Unlike Samitas and Tsakalos (2013), who used local headline stock market indices, we chose the MSCI indices because they are formulated consistently, such that cross-country comparisons can be achieved more accurately. Stock index returns are calculated by taking the difference of the natural logarithm of each stock index, multiplied by 100. All the data are collected from Thomson Reuters Datastream. Our sample period starts from 2 January 2003 and ends on 30 December 2011 and consists of 2,347 observations. The beginning date is set under the consideration that the initial turbulence caused by the introduction of the euro would have settled down by 2003.

Table 2.1 presents the summary statistics of the stock index return data for each of the five nations. It is notable that all the indices for the investigated countries, except that for Spain, experience negative average returns during the sample period. The stock index for Greece, the origin country of the European

Table 2.1 Summary statistics of stock index returns

Variable	Mean	Max	Min	SD	Skewness	Kurtosis	Jarque–Bera
GR	−0.0540	15.9580	−9.9490	1.9678	0.1493	8.3985	2858.7***
IR	−0.0340	13.3833	−17.7463	1.9222	−0.5562	12.4029	8767.2***
PT	−0.0043	10.3375	−10.7756	1.1765	0.0061	14.1827	12229.2***
IT	−0.0181	10.9855	−8.6276	1.4652	−0.0637	10.2225	5102.8***
ES	0.0125	14.5225	−10.1011	1.5228	0.2022	11.7719	7540.6***

Notes: Statistics for the difference of the logarithm of the daily stock indexes, multiplied by 100, are reported.

*** denotes statistical significance at the 1% level.

sovereign debt crisis, shows the highest volatility, represented by the standard deviation. Furthermore, the kurtosis level is high for all indices, suggesting leptokurtic distributions, which have heavier tails and acute peaks. The Jarque–Bera tests reject the null hypothesis of a normally distributed time series for all five indices. Further, we check whether the stock index return series are stationary, by conducting the ADF and Phillips–Perron tests. We confirm that no unit root processes are identified[4].

2.4. Empirical results

As explained in Section 2.2, we apply the univariate AR(1)-EGARCH(1,1) model to each stock index return series and then employ Engle and Kelly's (2012) DECO model to describe correlation dynamics. Table 2.2 depicts the estimated results. The coefficients of AR(1) terms in return equations are significant above the 5% level only in the case of Greece; however, all the parameters (ω, α_1, γ_1, and β_1) in variance equations based on EGARCH(1,1) models are significant at the 1% level. This implies that our model specification is appropriate, because the main objective of our study is to assess the correlation dynamics. Moreover, *p*-values of the Ljung–Box statistics, $Q(15)$ and $Q^2(15)$, indicate that no autocorrelation exists up to order 15 for standardized residuals and standard residuals squared.

Table 2.2 also indicates that the coefficients of a and b, which are the parameters in equation (6), are both highly significant. This shows that our derived equicorrelation estimates can infer correlation dynamics well, suggesting a substantial time-varying co-movement. The value of $a + b$ is close to unity, which implies a high level of persistency of the estimated equicorrelation.

The equicorrelation is plotted in Figure 2.1. Here, we should note that the DECO model yields the same correlation on a given day across all five indices and, hence, is markedly in contrast to the conventional DCC model which provides $n(n-1)/2 = 10$ correlations in total for each bivariate combination. This allows us to interpret the estimation results and draw implications more easily. As shown in Figure 2.1, the estimated dynamic equicorrelation exhibits high variability over time. The most striking point of the graph is that the correlation level becomes apparently higher after early 2007. In fact, the average correlation level was 0.586 between 2007 and 2011, as compared to 0.465 between 2003 and 2006. After 2007, equicorrelations have reached several peaks, such as in a) mid-March 2007, b) mid-August 2007, c) early February 2008, d) mid-September 2008, and e) early May 2010. Interestingly, these points in time correspond approximately to the occurrence of the following events, which highlight the aggravation of the financial crises: a) the suspension of shares in New Century Financial, one of the biggest subprime lenders in the US; b) the collapse of two Bear Stearns' hedge funds; c) the nationalization of Northern Rock by the British government; d) the bankruptcy of Lehman Brothers; and e) the first bailout package for Greece agreed by the IMF and EMU member countries. This means that the equicorrelations among GIIPS stock index returns soared under bear market conditions.

Table 2.2 Estimation of the AR-EGARCH model and the DECO model

First step: AR-EGARCH model

	GR		IR		PT		IT		ES	
	AR(1)-EGARCH(1,1)		AR(1)-EGARCH(1,1)		AR(1)-EGARCH(1,1)		AR(1)-EGARCH(1,1)		AR(1)-EGARCH(1,1)	
	Estimate	SE	Estimate	SE	Estimate	SE	Estimate	SE	Estimate	SE
Return equation										
φ_0	0.0612**	0.0249	0.0430**	0.0214	0.0452***	0.0149	0.0401**	0.0174	0.0405**	0.0186
φ_1	0.0406**	0.0202	0.0013	0.0197	0.0275	0.0201	-0.0160	0.0211	0.0069	0.0205
Variance equation										
ω	-0.1078***	0.0158	-0.1113***	0.0149	-0.1563***	0.0194	-0.0916***	0.0141	-0.1083***	0.0161
α_1	0.1535***	0.0213	0.1570***	0.0204	0.1978***	0.0249	0.1168***	0.0189	0.1470***	0.0213
γ_1	-0.0504***	0.0117	-0.0629***	0.0143	-0.0784***	0.0153	-0.1078***	0.0118	-0.1276***	0.0127
β_1	0.9893***	0.0031	0.9882***	0.0029	0.9769***	0.0052	0.9877***	0.0025	0.9805***	0.0037
GED param.	1.3973***	0.0586	1.3202***	0.0339	1.4113	0.0460	1.4280	0.0552	1.4275	0.0567
Q(15)	12.0700		9.6078		23.4330		12.1500		19.0220	
p-value	0.6740		0.8440		0.0750		0.6680		0.2130	
Q^2(15)	13.6070		7.8677		12.4230		12.2680		18.7700	
p-value	0.5560		0.9290		0.6470		0.6590		0.2240	

Second step: DECO model

Coefficient	Estimate	SE	Coefficient	Estimate	SE
a	0.0470***	0.0056	b	0.9331***	0.0088
Log-likelihood	-14282.9				

Notes: Q(15) and Q^2(15) are the Ljung–Box statistics up to the 15th order in standardized residuals and standardized residuals squared, respectively.

***, **, and * denote statistical significance at the 1%, 5%, and 10% levels, respectively.

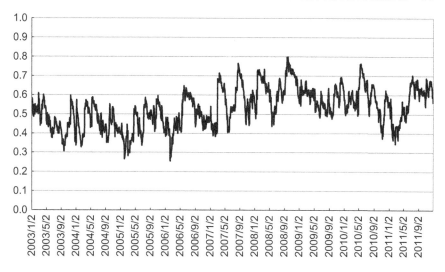

Figure 2.1 Estimated dynamic equicorrelation under the DECO model

With such a substantial increase in the level of equicorrelations identified after 2007, we are motivated to evaluate the potential impacts of the recent financial crises on the evolution of the estimated equicorrelations. This is because the need to pursue diversification is especially recognized in such periods of financial turmoil. In light of this, we apply an AR(1) model with dummy variables represented by

$$\hat{\rho}_t = \delta_0 + \delta_1 \hat{\rho}_{t-1} + \xi_1 D_{1,t} + \xi_2 D_{2,t} + e_t, \tag{7}$$

where $\hat{\rho}_t$ is the estimated dynamic equicorrelation derived from the DECO model, $D_{1,t}$ and $D_{2,t}$ signify the global financial crisis period (8 February 2007–4 November 2009) and the sovereign debt crisis period (5 November 2009–30 December 2011), respectively[5].

Table 2.3 reports the estimation results of the AR(1) model. The high value of adjusted R^2 (0.9522) demonstrates the appropriateness of our AR model specification. The coefficient on the lagged equicorrelation (δ_1) was highly significant and had a value close to 1, implying strong persistence of the estimated equicorrelation. We also confirm that both crisis dummy coefficients (ξ_1 and ξ_2) have positive signs and are statistically significant at the 1% level. Our empirical results show that both the global financial and sovereign debt crises significantly affected the degree of co-movement among the GIIPS stock markets. This is interesting because the origins of these two crises may differ—the global financial crisis originated in the US subprime loan market, whereas the onset of the European sovereign debt crisis was rooted in a small corner of the EMU financial markets, such as the Greek government bond markets. Nonetheless, as Eicher

Table 2.3 Dynamic equicorrelation and crisis periods

Coefficient	Estimate	SE
δ_0	0.0187***	0.0027
δ_1	0.9596***	0.0057
ξ_1 (Global financial crisis dummy)	0.0058***	0.0013
ξ_2 (European debt crisis dummy)	0.0044***	0.0013
Adjusted R^2	0.9522	

*** denotes statistical significance at the 1% level.

and Hielscher (2012) suggest, the identified significant impacts of both crises may be driven by the adverse effects of the US subprime loan crisis on many banks in the EMU. Owing to the crisis, the most vulnerable countries, such as GIIPS, experienced an economic downturn and had to resort to rescue programmes for their banks which were almost bankrupt. This resulted in investors becoming sceptical about sovereign default risks and the soaring government bond yields of those nations. Against this background, the herd behaviour of investors to sell their assets and convert them to cash, as seen during the global financial crisis, was also observed after the onset of the debt crisis. Thus, contagion effects may have been manifested in the GIIPS stock markets, in the form of the significant increase in the cross-market equicorrelation, although the debt crisis itself did not necessarily stem directly from the equity markets.

We are also interested in the economic factors that could potentially be associated with the movement of the estimated time-varying equicorrelation. The regression model we consider is

$$\hat{\rho}_t = \kappa_0 + \kappa_{rho}\,\hat{\rho}_{t-1} + \kappa_{EUR}EUR_{t-1} + \kappa_{INT}INT_{t-1} + \kappa_{SOV}SOV_{t-1} \\ + \kappa_{RIS}RIS_{t-1} + v_t, \tag{8}$$

where $\hat{\rho}_t$ is the estimated dynamic equicorrelation. Furthermore, the economic factors included are as follows: 1) the EUR/USD dollar exchange rate return (EUR_t); 2) the rate of change in the three-month euro interbank interest rate (INT_t); 3) the rate of change in the spread between the Greek and German 10-year Maastricht convergence bond yields (SOV_t); and 4) the rate of change in the spread between the US corporate (BBB) bond and the 10-year government bond to represent 'global risk aversion' (RIS_t).

Table 2.4 presents the estimated results for the above regression model in the entire period and in each of the three sub-periods. Overall, the explanatory power of the model is high, as reflected in the values of the adjusted R^2. The coefficient on the lagged equicorrelation (κ_{rho}) is also highly significant. Interestingly, among the four economic factors considered, only the coefficient on the global risk aversion variable was statistically significant at the 1% level in the entire period. Specifically, the coefficient was positively significant during both crisis periods,

Table 2.4 Dynamic equicorrelation and economic factors

Coefficient	(a) Entire period		(b) Pre-crisis period		(c) Global financial crisis period		(d) European debt crisis period	
	Estimate	SE	Estimate	SE	Estimate	SE	Estimate	SE
κ_0	0.0137***	0.0025	0.0214***	0.0043	0.0303***	0.0063	0.0218***	0.0061
κ_{rho}	0.9742***	0.0046	0.9537***	0.0092	0.9502***	0.0104	0.9623***	0.0104
κ_{EUR}	−0.0003	0.0007	0.0014	0.0012	0.0000	0.0012	−0.0025*	0.0013
κ_{INT}	−0.0003	0.0038	0.0011	0.0020	0.0012	0.0013	−0.0021	0.0014
κ_{SOV}	−0.0000	0.0001	0.0000	0.0001	−0.0000	0.0002	−0.0002	0.0002
κ_{RIS}	0.0010***	0.0003	0.0003	0.0003	0.0023***	0.0007	0.0012***	0.0004
Adjusted R^2	0.9520		0.9103		0.9245		0.9421	

***, **, and * denote statistical significance at the 1%, 5%, and 10% levels, respectively.

which implies that higher risk aversion among global investors led to higher co-movements among the GIIPS stock indices in times of market turbulence. This may be attributed to the herd behaviour of traders to sell off stocks of vulnerable countries simultaneously, triggering the contagion, which was represented as the regime shift of the stock market integration. Another interesting finding is that the coefficient on the EUR/USD exchange rate was negatively significant at the 10% level during the debt crisis, indicating that the euro devaluation in this period also increased the equicorrelation of the GIIPS stock markets. This illustrates the growing importance of the exchange rate in determining the GIIPS stock market integration in the period when concerns over sovereign risks of the peripheral economies appeared to trigger distrust of the common currency.

Our findings have valuable implications for global traders who are concerned about hedging and risk management across countries. Dynamic equicorrelation, which captures the time-varying correlation between all the assets concerned, can be a good indicator in constructing diversification strategies. The identified significant increase in dynamic equicorrelation of the GIIPS countries' stock indices implies that benefits from diversification diminished during not only the global financial crisis but also the sovereign debt crisis. Therefore, portfolio diversification among the stocks of those nations was not effective when it was most needed; that is, in times of market turbulence. This result is in contrast to that of Samitas and Tsakalos (2013), who investigated the dynamic correlation between the Greek and other EMU stock indices in a bivariate manner and concluded that contagion effects of the debt crisis were relatively limited.

Our empirical results are also relevant to policymakers who need to ensure properly functioning financial markets. In particular, they should be aware of the fact that contagion in the equity markets occurred even in the debt crisis, whose origin was in Greece's government bond (not equity) market. This highlights the importance of thoroughly assessing the causes of the financial turmoil. It also underscores the need for timely policy coordination across affected countries in order to prevent spillover effects. Based on our findings, the global risk aversion factor, which is expressed as the US corporate–government bond spread, should be especially closely monitored, because it may significantly affect the degree of stock market integration during financial crises.

2.5.   Conclusion

In this chapter, we examined the dynamic linkages of the MSCI stock indices in Greece, Ireland, Portugal, Italy, and Spain from 2 January 2003 to 30 December 2011. We employed Engle and Kelly's (2012) DECO model, which is an extension of Engle's (2002) DCC approach. The DECO methodology assumes that the time-varying correlation is equal across all assets at any given point of time; thus, it helps to avoid the difficulty of interpreting too many pairwise conditional correlations derived from the DCC technique. Using linear regression models, we also investigated the impacts of the two financial crises (the 2007–2009 global financial crisis and the European sovereign debt crisis) and several economic factors on the estimated dynamic equicorrelation.

Our empirical analysis revealed the following main findings. First, the estimated dynamic equicorrelation fluctuated substantially over time, with several peaks occurring especially after 2007. These peaks corresponded to the timing of events which represented the aggravation of financial crises. Second, both the global financial crisis and the European sovereign debt crisis significantly increased the dynamic equicorrelation of the GIIPS stock markets, implying the diminishing benefits of diversification strategies during crisis periods. Third, the global risk aversion factor (denoted by the US corporate–government bond spread) also significantly increased the co-movement of the GIIPS stock indices during the two crises. These results indicate that contagion, represented by the sudden increase in dynamic equicorrelation, may be driven by investors' herd behaviour of selling the stocks of affected nations which face a high level of uncertainty. Our results may be helpful not only for hedging and portfolio management by global investors but also for planning of coordinated efforts by policymakers to prevent financial market contagion.

Notes

1 Forbes and Rigobon (2002) contend that contagion is defined as a significant increase in cross-market linkages after shocks or crisis events.
2 See Nelson (1991) for details on the EGARCH model.
3 See Engle and Kelly (2012) for the log-likelihood expression related to the correlation under the DECO model.
4 The unit root test results are not reported here, but are available upon request.
5 We define 8 February 2007 and 5 November 2009 as the starting dates of the global credit crisis and the European sovereign debt crisis, respectively. The former date corresponds to HSBC's announcement regarding increasing its provision for bad debts, whereas the latter is related to Greece's disclosure that its fiscal deficit would be twice as large as the previously announced amount.

References

Bartram, S., Taylor, S., Wang, Y. (2007) The Euro and European financial market integration, *Journal of Banking and Finance*, **31**, 146–181.

Dajcman, S., Festic, M., Kavkler, A. (2012) European stock market comovement dynamics during some major financial market turmoils in the period 1997 to 2010 – a comparative DCC-GARCH and wavelet correlation analysis, *Applied Economics Letters*, **19**, 1249–1256.

Eicher, S., Hielscher, K. (2012) Does the ECB act as a lender of last resort during the subprime lending crisis?: Evidence from monetary policy reaction models, *Journal of International Money and Finance*, **31**, 552–568.

Engle, R. (2002) Dynamic conditional correlation: a simple class of multivariate generalized autoregressive conditional heteroskedasticity models, *Journal of Business & Economic Statistics*, **20**, 339–350.

Engle, R., Kelly, B. (2012) Dynamic equicorrelation, *Journal of Business & Economic Statistics*, **30**, 212–228.

Forbes, K., Rigobon, R. (2002) No contagion, only interdependence: measuring stock market comovements, *The Journal of Finance*, **57**, 2223–2262.

Grubel, H.G., Fadner, K. (1971) The interdependence of international equity markets, *The Journal of Finance*, **26**, 89–94.

Kearney, C., Poti, V. (2006) Correlation dynamics in European equity markets, *Research in International Business and Finance*, **20**, 305–321.

Kim, S.J., Moshirian, F., Wu, E. (2005) Dynamic stock market integration driven by the European Monetary Union: an empirical analysis, *Journal of Banking & Finance*, **29**, 2475–2502.

Longin, F., Solnik, B. (1995) Is the correlation in international equity returns constant: 1960–1990? *Journal of International Money and Finance*, **14**, 3–26.

Nelson, D.B. (1991) Conditional heteroskedasticity in asset returns: a new approach, *Econometrica*, **59**, 347–370.

Samitas, A., Tsakalos, I. (2013) How can a small country affect the European economy? The Greek contagion phenomenon, *Journal of International Financial Markets, Institutions and Money*, **25**, 18–32.

3 Co-movements among European exchange rates

3.1. Introduction

This chapter examines the co-movements of three daily US dollar (USD) exchange rates expressed in terms of the euro (EUR), British pound (GBP), and Swiss franc (CHF) during a sample period ranging from 1 January 1999 – when the euro was introduced – to 31 December 2010. The motivation for the study stems from the fact that assessing linkages among exchange rates has crucial implications. First, understanding this interdependence enables investors to assess how it affects international portfolio diversification that is exposed to risks of exchange rate fluctuations (e.g. Nikkinen et al., 2006). Second, the interdependence of exchange rates may also be relevant to monetary policymakers because it implies that exchange rates are influenced by common global factors, which cannot be controlled by local monetary policies alone (e.g. Ciner, 2011). In light of this, analysing time-varying linkages among currency markets – particularly since the launch of the euro – is intriguing because the introduction of this single currency, as argued by Mundell (1998), is regarded as one of the most important changes in the international monetary system.

A number of researchers have investigated the linkages among exchange rate series from the viewpoint of volatility spillovers since the seminal paper by Engle et al. (1990), who contend that exchange rate uncertainty arises not only from shocks in individual markets but also from shocks transmitted across markets. There are several recent examples of studies on this uncertainty in major European currencies. For example, Inagaki (2007) implements a cross-correlation function approach to examine volatility spillovers between the EUR and GBP and finds evidence of unidirectional causality-in-variance from the former to the latter. Kitamura (2010), employing the varying-correlation multivariate general autoregressive conditional heteroskedasticity (GARCH) model, analyses intraday volatility spillovers among the EUR, GBP, and CHF, finding evidence of volatility spillovers from the EUR to the latter two currencies. Furthermore, Nikkinen et al. (2006) apply the vector autoregressive model and Granger causality tests to expected future volatilities among the EUR, GBP, and CHF and find that the implied volatility of the EUR affects those of the GBP and CHF.

Another strand of research on the interdependence of exchange rates investigates time-varying correlations. For example, employing the DCC model developed by Engle (2002), Perez-Rodriguez (2006) finds that the correlations among the EUR, GBP, and CHF fluctuated significantly over the period 1999–2004 and that the dynamic correlation between the EUR and GBP was particularly high. Other recent studies apply copula models to assess the dependence structure of exchange rates. Using conditional copulas to model the joint density of the Deutsche mark and the Japanese yen against the US dollar, Patton (2006) finds that the correlation between the mark–dollar and yen–dollar exchange rates is higher when the currencies depreciate than when they appreciate. Moreover, Boero et al. (2011), who use copula models estimated by semi-parametric methods, identify major changes in the dependence structure of the euro–British pound and the euro–yen pairs since the launch of the euro. However, these previous studies do not address how the interdependence of exchange rates was affected by the recent European crisis.

The main objective of the present study, which complements and builds on the latter strand of research, is to explore the asymmetric dynamics in the correlations among exchange rates, as this remains underexplored in empirical research. From a theoretical viewpoint, as argued by Boero et al. (2011), asymmetric dependence – the different degrees of co-movements during periods of appreciation and depreciation – can perhaps be explained by currency portfolio rebalancing activities. That is, international investors tend to shift funds from other currencies to the USD when the USD is strong and from the USD to the next most important currencies when the USD is weak. Consequently, exchange rates display a higher degree of dependency during periods of depreciation against the USD (i.e. the former case) than appreciation against the USD (i.e. the latter case). Given this theoretical background, it would be interesting to examine empirically how the actual dependence structures of the three European exchange rates changed, particularly during the recent European crisis.

We make two primary contributions to the existing body of knowledge on this topic. First, we investigate the asymmetric behaviour of dynamic correlations among exchange rates using the multivariate asymmetric DCC (A-DCC) model proposed by Cappiello et al. (2006), being among the first to do so. This model is an extended version of the DCC model originally proposed by Engle (2002)[1]. Its ease of estimation makes the DCC approach suitable for the correlation of time series, modelled along with volatility, to change over time. However, the main modification introduced in the A-DCC model is to allow for conditional asymmetries in the covariance and correlation dynamics, thereby enabling researchers to examine the presence of asymmetric responses in correlations during periods of negative and positive shocks.

Second, this study assesses how the recent financial crisis in Europe influenced the estimated DCCs among the currency markets. Current empirical economics literature – for example, Chiang et al. (2007) – has demonstrated that significant increases in cross-market correlations tend to occur during market turbulence. We assess the existence of such increased correlations by modelling the estimated dynamic conditional correlation (obtained from the

A-DCC model) using autoregressive models with dummy variables. Specifically, we employ several crisis dummies to identify the most significant crisis period. While an increasing amount of research on the spread of financial crises has identified significant increases in DCCs in stock and bond returns, there have been few enquiries into the impacts on the co-movements of currency markets[2]. However, given that the recent financial turmoil has been accompanied by a credit crunch (i.e. the economy suffers from rising interest rates), this has confirmed that the crisis can affect both the money and foreign exchange markets, which are interconnected. Therefore, it is worthwhile examining how the recent financial turmoil in Europe has affected the dynamic interdependence of exchange rates.

The remainder of this paper is organized as follows. Section 3.2 presents the empirical methods. Section 3.3 offers a brief description of the data. Section 3.4 discusses the empirical results, and Section 3.5 concludes the paper.

3.2. Empirical methodology

We begin by specifying the conditional means in the following manner:

$$r_t = \phi_0 + \sum_{k=1}^{9} \phi_1 r_{t-k} + \varepsilon_t, \tag{1}$$

where $r_t = [r_{1t}, r_{2t}, r_{3t}]'$ is a 3×1 vector containing each foreign exchange returns series and $\varepsilon_t = [\varepsilon_{1t}, \varepsilon_{2t}, \varepsilon_{3t}]'$ is a 3×1 vector of the error terms with a generalized error distribution (GED). We fit the best of the univariate AR(k)-GARCH(1,1) models ($k = 1, 2, \ldots, 9$) to each time series based on the Schwarz Bayesian Information Criterion (SBIC). However, when all parameters in the lagged terms are found to be nonsignificant, we adopt the AR(0)-GARCH(1,1) model. Next, we specify the conditional variance-covariance matrix as

$$H_t = D_t R_t D_t, \tag{2}$$

where R_t is the time-varying correlation matrix and D_t is the diagonal matrix of the conditional standard deviations obtained from the univariate GARCH(1,1) models[3], with $\sqrt{h_{i,t}}$ on the ith diagonal:

$$h_{i,t} = \omega + \alpha_1 h_{i,t-1} + \beta_1 \varepsilon_{i,t-1}^2, \tag{3}$$

where $h_{i,t}$ is the conditional variance of the returns series. Note that the coefficients must satisfy the constraints in order to ensure positive and stable conditional variances; that is,

$$\alpha_1 > 0, \ \beta_1 > 0 \ \text{and} \ \alpha_1 + \beta_1 < 1. \tag{4}$$

Here, $\alpha_1 + \beta_1$ measures the persistence of the shocks to conditional variances.

By obtaining the conditional variance from Equation (3), we can examine the DCC. The evolution of the multivariate asymmetric generalized DCC (AG-DCC) model is provided by

$$Q_t = (\overline{P} - A'\overline{P}A - B'\overline{P}B - G'\overline{N}G) + A'z_{t-1}z'_{t-1}A + G'\eta_{t-1}\eta'_{t-1}G + B'Q_{t-1}B, \quad (5)$$

where A, B, and G are parameter matrices; $z_{i,t} = \varepsilon_{i,t}/\sqrt{h_{i,t}}$ are the standardized residuals from Equation (3); $\overline{P}$ and $\overline{N}$ are the unconditional correlation matrices of Z_t and η_t, and $\eta_t = I[z_t < 0]$ o z_t ($I[]$ is an indicator function that takes the value 1 if the argument is true and 0 otherwise; and "o" indicates a Hadamard product). The multivariate A-DCC(1,1) model we use in this study is regarded as a special case of the above AG-DCC(1,1) model when A, B, and G are replaced by scalars (a_1, b_1, and g_1). Within this setting, we calculate the time-varying correlation matrix using the following formula:

$$R_t = Q_t^{*-1}Q_tQ_t^{*-1}, \quad (6)$$

where Q_t^* is a diagonal matrix containing the square root of the diagonal entries of the covariance matrix, Q_t.

The final step in our procedure is to investigate whether there are significant changes in the dynamic correlations during the crisis. Here, following Kalbaska and Gatkowski (2012), we estimate the AR models in which the conditional correlations derived from Equation (6) are linked to their lagged values and several dummy variables, each representing a different definition of the European crisis period:

$$D\hat{C}C_t = \delta_0 + \delta_1 D\hat{C}C_{t-1} + \xi D_t^l + \lambda_t, \quad (7)$$

where $D\hat{C}C_t$ is the estimated conditional correlation and each D_t^l ($l = 1, 2, 3, 4$) is a dummy variable, defined as follows:

$D_t^1 = 1$ (after 9/8/2007), or 0 (elsewhere);

$D_t^2 = 1$ (after 15/9/2008), or 0 (elsewhere);

$D_t^3 = 1$ (after 5/11/2009), or 0 (elsewhere);

$D_t^4 = 1$ (after 23/4/2010), or 0 (elsewhere).

A key reason why we use several dummies is that there is apparently no consensus in economics literature on when the recent European crisis began. Here, D_t^1 represents the assumption that the outbreak of the crisis can be traced back to the occurrence of the global credit crisis, particularly when BNP Paribas, a major global investment bank, suspended its funds affected by the US subprime mortgage liabilities on 9 August 2007. Then, D_t^2 represents the assumption that the crisis began immediately after the bankruptcy of Lehman Brothers on

15 September 2008, and D_t^3 represents the assumption that the crisis began with the realization of the sovereign risk in Greece. In the latter case, the new Greek government announced its budget deficit amounting to 12.7% of GDP in November 2009, which was more than double the figure announced previously. Finally, D_t^4 represents the assumption that the crisis commenced when the Greek government requested an EU/IMF bailout package on 23 April 2010, which resulted in the bailout agreement of May 2010. The above specification allows us to conduct a sensitivity analysis and, thus, to verify the robustness of our empirical results (i.e. whether our definition of the crisis period affected the results regarding the existence of significant changes in correlations).

3.3. Data

The observation period ranges from 1 January 1999 to 31 December 2010[4]. We use daily USD exchange rates expressed in each of the three investigated foreign currencies (EUR, GBP, and CHF)[5]. These foreign currencies were selected because they are considered the most important European currencies, as measured by their daily trading volumes. The daily foreign exchange return is calculated as the first difference of the log-transformed prices, which is then multiplied by 100 to express it as a percentage. We use daily data not only to secure a sufficient number of observations to examine the recent European debt crisis but also to avoid the inefficiency that might arise if smaller samples are applied to a time-varying parameter method such as the A-DCC model.

Table 3.1 reports the descriptive statistics for our data set. The CHF exhibits the largest negative mean return, thereby suggesting that this currency (in the denominator) most appreciated against the USD (in the numerator). In contrast, the positive mean return for the GBP indicates the depreciation of the currency against the USD, on average. Note that the volatility (represented by standard deviation) of the CHF is the highest over the sample period. The relatively higher level of skewness for the GBP indicates that extreme changes tend to occur more frequently for this currency. The high values of kurtosis for all the currencies indicate the existence of fat tails in the return distribution. Furthermore, the

Table 3.1 Basic statistics on exchange rate returns

Variable	Mean (%)	Max (%)	Min (%)	SD	Skewness	Kurtosis	Jarque–Bera
EUR	−0.0043	3.8445	−4.6174	0.6399	−0.2249	5.7215	992.3***
GBP	0.0019	3.9187	−4.4737	0.5984	0.0350	7.6290	2,795.1***
CHF	−0.0124	4.4454	−5.4513	0.6779	−0.2754	5.9809	1,198.4***

Notes: The sample covers the period between 1 January 1999 and 31 December 2010 for 3,130 daily observations.

Statistics on the logarithmic difference of the daily currency data, multiplied by 100, are reported.

*** denotes statistical significance at the 1% level.

Jarque–Bera tests reject normality for all the exchange rate return series at the 1% significance level. The results of the augmented Dickey–Fuller unit root test confirm that all returns series are stationary[6].

3.4.   Empirical results

Specification of the conditional means and variances

The first step in our procedure is to fit the univariate AR(k)-GARCH(1,1) models to each series of the foreign exchange rates. As shown in Table 3.2, which reports the estimation results of the AR-GARCH models, we selected the AR(0)-GARCH(1,1) model for all the exchange return series. The variance equations of each model display a good fit to the data and, thus, are considered to provide support for our selection of GARCH models to capture the conditional variances. Indeed, all the parameters in the equations are significant at the 10% level. Moreover, the *p*-values of the Ljung–Box statistics, $Q(12)$ and $Q^2(12)$, for all three foreign exchange rates suggest there is no autocorrelation up to order 12 for standardized residuals and standardized residuals squared[7]. However, the constant parameters in the conditional mean equations were nonsignificant. Since our analysis focuses on the dynamics of the correlations among the exchange rate returns, the well-fitted variance equations described above led us to conclude that our AR-GARCH models fit the data reasonably well.

Table 3.2 Empirical results of univariate AR-GARCH models

	EUR		GBP		CHF	
	AR(0)-GARCH(1,1)		AR(0)-GARCH(1,1)		AR(0)-GARCH(1,1)	
	Estimate	SE	Estimate	SE	Estimate	SE
Conditional mean equation						
φ_0	−0.0086	0.0097	−0.0095	0.0086	−0.0033	0.0107
Conditional variance equation						
ω	0.0014*	0.0008	0.0022***	0.0008	0.0028**	0.0013
α_1	0.0277***	0.0050	0.0381***	0.0065	0.0248***	0.0050
β_1	0.9692***	0.0056	0.9555***	0.0075	0.9692***	0.0065
GED parameter	1.4711***	0.0519	1.4992***	0.0522	1.4645***	0.0473
$Q(12)$	11.1770		13.5340		13.4050	
p-value	0.5140		0.3310		0.3400	
$Q^2(12)$	14.4830		4.8265		14.1520	
p-value	0.2710		0.9640		0.2910	

Notes: $Q(12)$ and $Q^2(12)$ are the Ljung–Box statistics up to the 12th order in the standardized residuals and standardized residuals squared, respectively.

***, **, and * denote statistical significance at the 1%, 5%, and 10% levels, respectively.

Multivariate asymmetric DCC framework

The next step is to estimate the multivariate A-DCC models. Table 3.3 indicates the results of the principal component analysis for the exchange rate returns series. The largest principal component explains 81% of the total variation, while the explanatory power of the principal components declines substantially if we subtract this component. This result implies that, among the three foreign exchange rates investigated, one common factor drives a substantial proportion of the total variation. This first common component can be interpreted as a general underlying trend for the currencies, presumably driven by increased economic and financial convergence, which is believed to have arisen from the facilitation of regional trade and the elimination of capital control in European countries. Table 3.3 also indicates that the contemporaneous correlations between each pair of exchange rates are high, with the EUR–CHF pair having the highest correlation of 0.89. In Figure 3.1, we plot the rolling correlations between each pair of exchange rates, with time spans of three months, six months, one year, and two years. Interestingly, we find more fluctuations in the rolling correlations in downward directions between each pair, particularly after 2007, regardless of the time span. Moreover, we detect particularly sharp decreases in the correlations between the CHF–EUR and GBP–CHF pairs after 2010.

The results of the A-DCC estimation are presented in Table 3.4. Overall, we find that the A-DCC model seems to be specified reasonably well. Indeed, the estimates of the parameter of standardized residuals (a_1) and of innovations in the dynamics of the conditional correlation matrix (b_1) are significant at the 1% level. Most notably, the estimate of the parameter of the asymmetric term (g_1) is significant at the 10% level, thereby providing evidence of an asymmetric response in correlations. In other words, the conditional correlation among the currencies exhibits a higher dependency when it is driven by negative innovations to changes (joint appreciation of the European currencies[8]) than it is by

Table 3.3 Principal components analysis of exchange rate returns

Variable	Eigenvalue	Cumulative value	Proportion of variances	Cumulative proportion
First principal component	2.4350	2.4350	0.8117	0.8117
Second principal component	0.4655	2.9005	0.1552	0.9668
Third principal component	0.0995	3.0000	0.0332	1.0000

Ordinary correlations	EUR	GBP	CHF
EUR	1.0000	–	–
GBP	0.6721	1.0000	–
CHF	0.8907	0.5769	1.0000

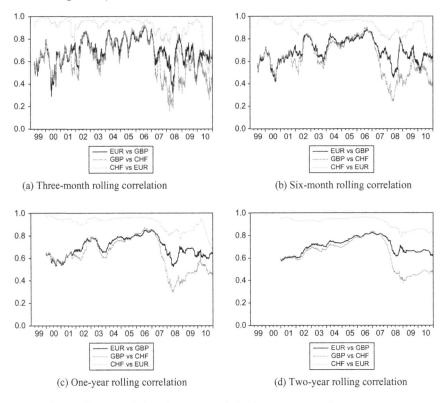

(a) Three-month rolling correlation

(b) Six-month rolling correlation

(c) One-year rolling correlation

(d) Two-year rolling correlation

Figure 3.1 Rolling correlations between each foreign currency pair

Table 3.4 Dynamic conditional correlation (DCC) estimates of exchange rate returns

Coefficient	Estimate	SE	Coefficient	Estimate	SE	Coefficient	Estimate	SE
a_1	0.0256***	0.0037	b_1	0.9669***	0.0052	g_1	0.0088*	0.0053
Log-likelihood	−4307.0							

*** and * denote statistical significance at the 1% and 10% levels, respectively.

positive innovations (joint depreciation). This result is rather intriguing because it suggests that the reasons for the identified asymmetric correlation differ from the theoretical explanation of the 'currency portfolio rebalancing' hypothesis described in Section 3.1, which argues that exchange rates tend to display a higher degree of co-movement during periods of depreciation than appreciation against the USD. In order to examine what has driven the asymmetric pattern in the correlation revealed in our analysis, we examine the DCC estimates in each pair of exchange rates more closely, as follows.

Figure 3.2 plots the estimated DCCs between each pair. First, the time path of the DCC series fluctuates over the entire sample period for all pairs, thereby

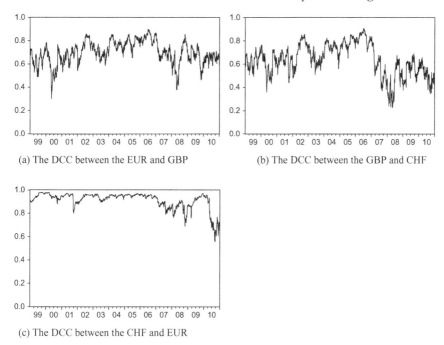

(a) The DCC between the EUR and GBP

(b) The DCC between the GBP and CHF

(c) The DCC between the CHF and EUR

Figure 3.2 Dynamic conditional correlations between each foreign currency pair

suggesting that the assumption of constant correlations may not be appropriate. This result is generally in line with previous studies, such as Perez-Rodriguez (2006). Second, the estimated DCCs between all pairs remain at a relatively high level (i.e. above 0.6) before 2007. This implies the progress of a substantial degree of market integration, which has occurred since the inception of the euro. Third, the DCC series between the GBP–CHF and CHF–EUR pairs show sharp declines during the financial crisis after 2007, with that of the CHF–EUR pair facing further declines after late 2009 in particular. Such evidence of declines in the DCCs among these pairs of exchange rates contrasts with the findings of previous research, which has tended to show increases in the correlations during periods of financial turmoil in the case of the DCCs of stock returns (e.g. see Yiu et al., 2010).

These behaviours of the estimated DCC series may provide an explanation for the identified asymmetries in the correlations among the three exchange rates. During the pre-crisis period, the common factor, driven by increases in the convergence of the economies and financial markets in the European nations, may have caused all three currencies (EUR, GBP, and CHF) to appreciate against the USD, thereby triggering the observed high level of dependence among the exchange rates. In contrast, after the occurrence of the financial turmoil in Europe, market participants became more risk-averse and the role of the CHF as a safe-haven currency[9] strengthened. As a result, the level of depreciation against the

USD may have been different between the CHF and other two currencies, thereby displaying a decline in dependence between the GBP–CHF and CHF–EUR pairs. Such a hypothesis on the asymmetric correlations motivated us to investigate the impacts of the crisis. In particular, by applying AR models with dummy variables to the estimated DCCs, we examined whether the crisis significantly decreased the dynamic correlation rather than increased it.

AR models with crisis dummies

The final step is to estimate the evolution of the estimated DCCs using AR(1) models with several crisis dummy variables, as described previously. Table 3.5 reports the estimation results. Regardless of our definition of the crisis period,

Table 3.5 Estimation of AR models for the estimated DCC coefficients: sensitivity analysis

Panel A (Crisis period started after 9/8/2007)

Coefficient	EUR vs. GBP		GBP vs. CHF		CHF vs. EUR	
	Estimate	SE	Estimate	SE	Estimate	SE
δ_0	0.011178***	0.002291	0.010887***	0.002307	0.007014***	0.002264
δ_1	0.984405***	0.003157	0.984161***	0.003280	0.992519***	0.002401
ξ	–0.001034	0.000676	–0.003110***	0.000992	–0.000908**	0.000380
Adjusted R^2	0.971427		0.980403		0.989249	

Panel B (Crisis period started after 15/9/2008)

Coefficient	EUR vs. GBP		GBP vs. CHF		CHF vs. EUR	
	Estimate	SE	Estimate	SE	Estimate	SE
δ_0	0.010326***	0.002181	0.007513***	0.001844	0.005638***	0.002025
δ_1	0.985398***	0.003053	0.988650***	0.002721	0.993910***	0.002170
ξ	–0.000709	0.000748	–0.001914**	0.000942	–0.000786**	0.000393
Adjusted R^2	0.971414		0.980367		0.994990	

Panel C (Crisis period started after 5/11/2009)

Coefficient	EUR vs. GBP		GBP vs. CHF		CHF vs. EUR	
	Estimate	SE	Estimate	SE	Estimate	SE
δ_0	0.010152***	0.002204	0.006619***	0.001750	0.007109***	0.001996
δ_1	0.985514***	0.003089	0.989725***	0.002631	0.992324***	0.002154
ξ	–0.000451	0.001009	–0.001638	0.001215	–0.001819***	0.000521
Adjusted R^2	0.971408		0.980353		0.989271	

Panel D (Crisis period started after 23/4/2010)

Coefficient	EUR vs. GBP		GBP vs. CHF		CHF vs. EUR	
	Estimate	SE	Estimate	SE	Estimate	SE
δ_0	0.010106***	0.002158	0.006899***	0.001736	0.012577***	0.002472
δ_1	0.985585***	0.003041	0.989304***	0.002627	0.986401***	0.002668
ξ	−0.000818	0.001257	−0.002928*	0.001534	−0.004140***	0.000816
Adjusted R^2	0.971410		0.980364		0.989318	

***, **, and * denote statistical significance at the 1%, 5%, and 10% levels, respectively.

the coefficients of the constant terms (δ_0) and the AR(1) terms (δ_1)[10] are both significant for all three pairs at the 5% significance level. Moreover, the high values of the adjusted R^2 suggest that the regression models are suitably specified in all cases.

Here, it is worth noting three interesting observations in terms of the coefficients of the crisis dummies (ξ). First, for the CHF–EUR pair, the coefficients of the European crisis dummies are negative and significant at the 5% level in all four cases. In particular, they are most significant (i.e. at the 1% level) after the increase in the Greek sovereign risk in November 2009 (Panel C) and after the problems in Greece worsened in April 2010 (Panel D). This suggests that the Greek debt crisis significantly lowered the DCC for this pair. Second, in the case of the GBP–CHF pair, the coefficients of the crisis dummies are negative and significant at the 10% level in all cases, except Panel C. In addition, they are most significant (i.e. at the 1% level) with the highest absolute value of the dummy coefficient after the occurrence of the global credit crunch in August 2007 (Panel A). This implies that there was a more significant decline in the DCC for the GBP–CHF pair after the global subprime loan crisis than there was after the European debt crisis. Third, for the EUR–GBP pair, the coefficients of the European crisis dummies are nonsignificant, even at the 10% level, in all four cases. This indicates that the crisis did not have a significant impact on the interrelationship between these two exchange rates at all, regardless of our definition of the onset of the crisis.

The findings on the significance of crisis dummy coefficients may provide additional support to our explanation for asymmetries in the correlations of the exchange rates provided previously. An increased level of risk due to the onset of the global subprime loan crisis resulted in enhancing the role of the CHF as a safe-haven currency. The GBP was hit harder by the global credit crisis than the CHF, perhaps owing to the close economic and financial ties between the United Kingdom and United States, where the credit crisis originated. The CHF also served as a safe-haven currency when the EUR was devalued after the deterioration of public finances in Greece and the associated increases in Greek government bond yields, as demonstrated by Kasimati (2011). The differing degrees of vulnerability of these European currencies to the financial crises triggered a lower dependency during periods of depreciation when compared to periods of joint appreciation driven by the common factor in the pre-crisis period. This led us to identify the asymmetry in the correlations.

Our empirical results are useful for both international investors and monetary authorities. On the one hand, in terms of portfolio risk management, global investors should become more aware of the increased risk exposure of the frequent fluctuations in the correlations between the exchange rates during the recent European financial crisis. On the other hand, they may find more diversification opportunities associated with the lower degree of dependency between the exchange rates during the crisis than during the pre-crisis period. For policymakers, the high level of interdependence – as evident among the three currencies during the pre-crisis period – implies that it would be difficult to control exchange rates through local monetary policies alone because of the increased economic and financial integration. Furthermore, understanding the evolution of the dependence among exchange rates is critical for determining whether and how policymakers should pursue foreign exchange market interventions[11]. In fact, the Swiss central bank's announcement of setting an exchange rate target against the EUR in September 2011, and its subsequent series of interventions, may reflect their concern over the sharp appreciation of the CHF (i.e. lower DCC between the CHF–EUR pair) associated with higher risk aversion of market participants as the European debt crisis intensified.

3.5.   Conclusion

In this study, we examined the time-varying linkages among daily USD exchange rates, expressed in three major European currencies (EUR, GBP, and CHF). Specifically, we used the multivariate asymmetric DCC approach put forward by Cappiello et al. (2006) for the sample period from January 1999 to December 2010. The study assessed how the recent European crisis influenced the estimated dynamic correlations by modelling them using AR models with dummy variables. Employing several crisis dummies enabled us to conduct a sensitivity analysis with regard to whether the definition of the European crisis period may have caused significant changes in the dynamic correlations.

The empirical results revealed the following four principal aspects. First, our analysis found evidence of an asymmetric response in the correlation among the three exchange returns. That is, we found a higher degree of interdependence during periods of appreciation than depreciation against the USD. This interesting finding may be explained by both 1) the increased economic and financial convergence leading to a high dependency in correlations before 2007; and 2) the emerging role of the CHF as a safe-haven currency, thereby having a different level of vulnerability (lower dependency in correlation) than the other European currencies after the onset of the recent financial crisis. Second, the estimated dynamic correlation for the CHF–EUR pair was found to decrease significantly, particularly after the Greek sovereign risk increased in November 2009 and after Greece's request for an EU/IMF bailout package in April 2010. Third, there was a significant decrease in the estimated dynamic correlation for the GBP–CHF pair, particularly after the onset of the global credit crisis in August 2007, which caused financial shocks to the GBP and CHF in different ways. Fourth, there were no significant impacts of the crisis in the case of correlations in the EUR–GBP pair, regardless of the definition of the crisis period.

Our findings are of great relevance to international investors when making financial decisions on managing their risk exposure to exchange rate fluctuations and on taking advantage of potential diversification opportunities owing to the lower dependence among exchange rates. The empirical results also have important implications for monetary policymakers, who need to be aware of the difficulty of exerting control over exchange rates only through local monetary policies at times of increased dependence, and deciding on the timing and extent of foreign exchange rate interventions.

Notes

1   Several previous empirical studies have used Engle's (2002) DCC model or the A-DCC model of Cappiello et al. (2006) to analyse stock or bond returns (e.g. Yang, 2005; Savva et al., 2009; Yiu et al., 2010; Kenourgios et al., 2011; Kenourgios and Padhi, 2012; Yang et al., 2012; Zhang and Li, 2014).
2   See Dungey and Martin (2007) for a detailed list of related financial crisis literature.
3   See Bollerslev (1986) for details on the GARCH model.
4   In September 2011, the Swiss central bank announced an exchange rate target against the EUR, and the central bank intervened heavily when the threshold was reached. Our sample period, ending 31 December 2010, eliminates the potential impacts of such interventions.
5   These data are sourced from WM/Reuters, provided by Thomson Reuters DataStream.
6   The results of the unit root tests are available upon request.
7   See Ljung and Box (1978).
8   Please note that these currencies are in the denominator and hence their appreciation results in negative returns in our definition of the exchange rates.
9   See Renaldo and Soderlind (2010) for details on the background of the role of a safe-haven currency. They define a safe-haven currency as one that benefits from risk aversion by market participants and appreciates when the risk soars. Their empirical analysis demonstrates that the CHF has characteristics of being a safe-haven currency (as does the EUR, although weaker), whilst the GBP is not considered a safe-haven currency at all.
10 The coefficients of the AR(1) term take values close to unity, thereby indicating a strong persistence in the correlations among the exchange rates studied. Note that the persistence of the dynamic conditional correlations tends to be overestimated if structural breaks exist. One way to avoid this may be adding more dummy variables, such as those signifying changes in the monetary policies adopted by central banks. In this study, we did not pursue this approach, instead concentrating on analysing the impacts of events related to the European financial crises. Analysing the impacts of policy interventions remains a subject for future research.
11 See Sarno and Taylor (2001) for more details on previous literature on foreign exchange market interventions.

References

Boero, G., Silvapulle, P., Tursunalieva, A. (2011) Modelling the bivariate dependence structure of exchange rates before and after the introduction of the euro: A semi-parametric approach, *International Journal of Finance & Economics*, **16**, 357–374.

Bollerslev, T. (1986) Generalized autoregressive conditional heteroskedasticity, *Journal of Econometrics*, **52**, 5–59.

Cappiello, L., Engle, R., Sheppard, K. (2006) Asymmetric dynamics in the correlations of global equity and bond returns, *Journal of Financial Econometrics*, **4**, 557–572.

Chiang, T.C., Jeon, B.N., Li, H. (2007) Dynamic correlation analysis of financial contagion: Evidence from Asian markets, *Journal of International Money and Finance*, **26**, 1206–1228.

Ciner, C. (2011) Information transmission across currency futures market: Evidence from frequency domain tests, *International Review of Financial Analysis*, **20**, 134–139.

Dungey, M., Martin, V. (2007) Unravelling financial market linkages during crises, *Journal of Applied Econometrics*, **22**, 89–119.

Engle, R. (2002) Dynamic conditional correlation: A simple class of multivariate generalized autoregressive conditional heteroskedasticity models, *Journal of Business and Economic Statistics*, **20**, 339–350.

Engle, R., Ito, T., Lin, W.L. (1990) Meteor showers or heat waves? Heteroskedastic intra daily volatility in the foreign exchange market, *Econometrica*, **58**, 525–542.

Inagaki, K. (2007) Testing for volatility spillover between the British pound and the euro, *Research in International Business and Finance*, **21**, 161–174.

Kalbaska, A., Gatkowski, M. (2012) Eurozone sovereign contagion: Evidence from the CDS market (2005–2010), *Journal of Economic Behavior & Organization*, **83**, 657–673.

Kasimati, E. (2011) Did the climb on the Greek sovereign spreads cause the devaluation of euro? *Applied Economics Letters*, **18**, 851–854.

Kenourgios, D., Samitas, A., Paltalidis, N. (2011) Financial crises and stock market contagion in a multivariate time-varying asymmetric framework, *Journal of International Financial Markets, Institutions, and Money*, **21**, 92–106.

Kenourgios, D., Padhi, P. (2012) Emerging markets and financial crises: Regional, global or isolated shocks? *Journal of Multinational Financial Management*, **22**, 24–28.

Kitamura, Y. (2010) Testing for intraday interdependence and volatility spillover among the euro, the pound and Swiss franc markets, *Research in International Business and Finance*, **24**, 158–171.

Ljung, G., Box, G. (1978) On a measure of lack of fit in time series models, *Biometrika*, **66**, 265–270.

Mundell, R. (1998) What the euro means for the dollar and the international monetary system, *Atlantic Economic Journal*, **26**, 227–237.

Nikkinen, J., Sahlstrom, P., Vahamaa, S. (2006) Implied volatility linkages among major European currencies, *Journal of International Financial Markets, Institutions & Money*, **16**, 87–103.

Patton, A.J. (2006) Modelling asymmetric exchange rate dependence, *International Economic Review*, **47**, 527–556.

Renaldo, A., Soderlind, P. (2010) Safe haven currencies, *Review of Finance*, **14**, 385–407.

Sarno, L., Taylor, M.P. (2001) Official intervention in the foreign exchange market: Is it effective and, if so, how does it work? *Journal of Economic Literature*, **39**, 839–868.

Savva, C.S., Osborn, D.R., Gill, L. (2009) Spillovers and correlations between U.S. and major European stock markets: The role of the euro, *Applied Financial Economics*, **19**, 1595–1604.

Yang, J., Zhou, Y., Leung, W.K. (2012) Asymmetric correlation and volatility dynamics among stock, bond, and securitized real estate markets, *The Journal of Real Estate Finance and Economics*, **45**, 491–521.

Yang, S.Y. (2005) A DCC analysis of international stock market correlations: The role of Japan on the Asian four tigers, *Applied Financial Economics Letters*, **1**, 89–93.

Yiu, M.S., Ho, W.A., Choi, D.F. (2010) Dynamic correlation analysis of financial contagion in Asian markets in global financial turmoil, *Applied Financial Economics*, **20**, 345–354.

Zhang, B., Li, X.M. (2014). Has there been any change in the comovement between the Chinese and U.S. stock markets, *International Review of Economics and Finance*, **29**, 525–536.

Part II

How were causalities among financial markets altered by the crisis?

4 The causality between Greek sovereign bond yields and southern European banking sector equity returns

4.1. Introduction

Since the onset of the recent Greek sovereign debt crisis, bank managers and monetary authorities in Greece and in neighbouring countries such as Portugal, Italy, and Spain have become more cautious about the relationships between their bank stock returns and changes in Greek government bond yields. Their imminent concern seems to stem from the fact that these countries hold considerable amounts of Greek sovereign bonds. Indeed, according to the results of the stress test conducted by the European Banking Authority in July 2011, the exposure of banks in Greece, Portugal, Italy, and Spain to Greek sovereign debt amounts to 54.4, 1.4, 1.4, and 0.4 billion euro, respectively. This degree of exposure implies that even a moderate level of haircuts on these debts might cause significant losses in the banking sectors of those countries. This conclusion suggests that it is worthwhile investigating the potential causality between Greek government bond yields and the bank stock returns of these four Mediterranean countries.

Previous studies have shown that the causal linkage between bank stock returns and bond yields can, theoretically, display different directions and signs. Present value models imply that stock prices fall when long-term interest rates increase. Nonetheless, as Shiller and Beltratti (1992) contend, a positive relationship between stock prices and long-term interest rates can also exist when changes in interest rates carry information about the outlook for future dividends. Moreover, we can consider the opposite causality, namely from stock returns to long-term interest rates. As Alaganar and Bhar (2003) argue, because stock markets are forward-looking in nature, current stock prices may reflect expectations about future interest rates. This is particularly true for banking sectors, whose profit levels can be closely related to interest rates.

Another stream of research has analysed the relationship between bank stock returns and interest rates empirically. Earlier studies, which typically employed a two-index model (i.e. interest rates and market factors) under the assumption of constant variance, yielded mixed results in terms of the causality between them. Several studies have contended that interest rates do not significantly affect the stock returns of financial institutions (e.g. Lloyd and Shick 1977; Chance and Lane 1980). In contrast, Flannery and James (1984) and Bae (1990) provide evidence of the negative impact of interest rates on banking sector stock returns. As Bae (1990) points out, varied constructions of interest rate series may be one reason for such mixed results.

Moreover, recent studies of the relationship between interest rates and bank stock returns have assumed time-varying conditional variance. Based on this assumption, they have either adopted different classes of the autoregressive conditional heteroskedasticity (ARCH) models developed by Engle (1982) or the generalized autoregressive conditional heteroskedasticity (GARCH) models proposed by Bollerslev (1986). Song (1994) was among the first to use an ARCH-type model to demonstrate that the time-varying risk measures of interest rates are incorporated in the pricing of US banking sector stocks. Elyasiani and Mansur (1998) employ a GARCH-in-mean (GARCH-M) model to identify the negative effects of long-term interest rates and their volatilities on both the means and variances of US bank stock returns. Tai (2000), using three different approaches, including a multivariate GARCH-M model, confirms the significant impacts of interest rates, the world market, and exchange rate risks on US bank stock returns. Using a multivariate GARCH model, Elyasiani and Mansur (2004) also find evidence of the significant influence of short-term and long-term interest rates and their volatilities on US bank stock returns. Verma and Jackson (2008) extend the latter study by employing a multivariate exponential GARCH (EGARCH) model to demonstrate the asymmetric influence of positive and negative interest rate changes on US bank stock returns. Their results show that bank equity returns are more sensitive to negative than positive changes in interest rates.

Another approach in empirical literature is to employ cross-correlation function (CCF) methodologies, primarily to investigate the short-term dynamics in the relationship between interest rates and bank stock returns. Alaganar and Bhar (2003) find support for a two-way information flow between interest rates and financial sector returns of G7 countries, based on the causality-in-mean and causality-in-variance tests suggested by Cheung and Ng (1996). One of the key advantages of this approach is that it can detect the direction of causality and the lead-lag structure of the causality at the variance and mean levels. It is important to analyse causality-in-variance because volatility contains useful data on information flows, as Ross (1989) points out. In addition, Engle et al. (1990) attribute the volatility movement of asset price changes to the time necessary for investors to process new information.

The present study uses daily data from January 2007 to June 2011 to examine the causality-in-variance and causality-in-mean between long-term government bond yields in Greece and the banking sector stock returns of four southern European countries, namely Greece, Portugal, Italy, and Spain. Thus, we extend the existing literature on the relationship between interest rates and bank stock returns in the following two ways. First, ours is one of the few studies to assess the two-way, cross-border spillover of information flows between bond yields and bank stock returns. Most previous studies have investigated only within-country transmission effects. Indeed, we are among the first to study how the recent Greek sovereign debt crisis might affect the relationship between Greek long-term government bonds and banking sector stocks in neighbouring countries. Second, we use the CCF approach recently developed by Hong (2001). This methodology improves on Cheung and Ng's (1996) model, which is constrained by uniform weights for each lag, making no distinction between recent and distant cross-correlations. The results of our study are relevant for policymakers as well as bank managers in the affected countries who intend to monitor and prevent cross-country spillover effects between sovereign bond yields and bank stock returns.

The remainder of this chapter is organized as follows. Section 4.2 presents the empirical framework used in this study, followed by an explanation of our dataset in Section 4.3. Then, Section 4.4 reports our findings from the causality tests. Finally, Section 4.5 concludes the chapter.

4.2. Empirical methodology

This study employs the two-step CCF methodology proposed by Hong (2001). In the first step, we fit a univariate model to each data series, allowing for a time-varying conditional mean and variance. Compared with the research designs of Elyasiani and Mansur (1998) and Alaganar and Bhar (2003), who apply GARCH(1,1) models, we select the best of the AR(k)-EGARCH(p,q) models, shown as follows[1]:

$$\Delta r_t = a_0 + \sum_{i=1}^{k} a_i \Delta r_{t-i} + \varepsilon_t, \quad E_{t-1}(\varepsilon_t) = 0, \quad E_{t-1}(\varepsilon_t^2) = \sigma^2, \tag{1}$$

$$\log(\sigma_t^2) = \omega + \sum_{i=1}^{q} (\alpha_i |z_{t-i}| + \gamma_i z_{t-i}) + \sum_{i=1}^{p} \beta_i \log(\sigma_{t-i}^2), \tag{2}$$

where $z_t = \varepsilon_t / \sigma_t$ has a normal distribution with zero mean and unit variance, and Δr_t represents the first differences of the natural logarithm of each time series. We select $k(= 1, 2, ..., 10)$, $p(= 1, 2)$, and $q(= 1, 2)$ based on the Schwarz Bayesian information criterion and use residual diagnostics to avoid autocorrelation.

Using the EGARCH model for this purpose is appropriate for the following two reasons. First, since the logarithmic form of the model ensures the nonnegativity of the conditional variance, we are not constrained by the signs of the coefficients, unlike in the GARCH framework. Second, and more importantly, the coefficients of the ARCH terms in the EGARCH model capture the asymmetric effects caused by positive and negative shocks. This may provide a good fit to test the proposed relationships because in the actual banking sector stock (or government bond) markets, the shocks to volatilities differ depending on whether stock price returns (or bond yields) increase or decrease.

In the second step, we conduct the causality-in-variance and causality-in-mean tests using weighted CCF values[2]. Previously, a typical approach to investigate volatility spillovers was to apply a GARCH model, simultaneously modelling more than two time series. One drawback of using a multivariate GARCH framework is that many parameters must be estimated, which generates a degree of computational complexity. Moreover, uncertainty can be created in terms of first- and second-moment dynamics, as the time series are likely to interact. In contrast, the CCF approach put forward by Cheung and Ng (1996) avoids these issues by employing a two-step procedure. Here, each time series is fitted to a univariate model and then the null hypothesis of no causality-in-variance is tested using the CCF values of the squared standardized residuals. This test makes no distributional assumptions on innovation processes and, thus, tends to display greater power than traditional Granger causality tests.

Let X_t and Y_t be two stationary time series. Then, we denote two information sets,

$$I_t = \{X_{t-j}; j \geq 0\} \text{ and } J_t = \{X_{t-j}, Y_{t-j}; j \geq 0\}. \tag{3}$$

We can conclude that Y_t causes X_t in variance if

$$E[(X_t - \mu_{X,t})^2 \mid I_{t-1}] \neq E[(X_t - \mu_{X,t})^2 \mid J_{t-1}], \tag{4}$$

where $\mu_{X,t}$ represents the mean of X_t conditional on I_t.

In order to test for the null hypothesis of no causality-in-variance during the first M lags, Cheung and Ng (1996) developed an S-statistic, which is asymptotically robust to distribution assumptions, as follows:

$$S = T \sum_{i=1}^{M} \hat{\rho}_{uv}^2(i) \xrightarrow{L} \chi^2(M), \tag{5}$$

where

$$\hat{\rho}_{uv}(i) = \{c_{uu}(0)c_{vv}(0)\}^{-1/2} c_{uv}(i), \tag{6}$$

$$c_{uv}(j) = T^{-1} \sum_{t=1}^{T-j} (\hat{u}_t - \bar{u})(\hat{v}_{t+j} - \bar{v}) \text{ for } j \geq 0,$$

$$= T^{-1} \sum_{t=1}^{T-j} (\hat{u}_{t-j} - \bar{u})(\hat{v}_t - \bar{v}) \text{ for } j < 0, \tag{7}$$

$$u_t = (X_t - \mu_{X,t})^2 / h_{X,t}, \tag{8}$$

$$v_t = (Y_t - \mu_{Y,t})^2 / h_{Y,t}. \tag{9}$$

Here, $c_{uu}(0)$ and $c_{vv}(0)$ represent the sample variances of disturbances, u_t and v_t. Further, $h_{i,t}$ represents a conditional variance of a GARCH(p, q) model and T is the sample size.

A key shortcoming of this S-statistic is that it places a uniform weight on each lag, with no differentiation between recent and distant cross-correlations. Therefore, the S-statistic is not consistent with the intuition that more recent information should be weighted more heavily. To avoid this issue, Hong (2001) modified and extended the CCF methodology by developing the following Q-statistic to test for one-sided causality[3]:

$$Q = \{T \sum_{j=1}^{T-1} k^2 (j/M) \hat{\rho}_{uv}(j) - C_{1T}(k)\} / \{2D_{1T}(k)\}^{1/2}, \tag{10}$$

where

$$C_{1T}(k) = \sum_{j=1}^{T-1} (1 - j/T) k^2 (j/M),$$

$$D_{1T}(k) = \sum_{j=1}^{T-1} (1 - j/T)\{1 - (j+1)/T\} k^4 (j/M),$$

$$k(z) = \begin{cases} 1, & |z| \leq 1, \\ 0, & otherwise. \end{cases}$$

Hong (2001) shows that

$Q \rightarrow N(0,1)$ *in distribution.*

If the Q-statistic is larger than the upper-tailed $N(0,1)$ critical values, we reject the null hypothesis of no causality-in-variance during the first M lags. Further, because this test does not rely on distributional assumptions, the specification of the innovation process is more flexible. A similar process could be employed for causality-in-mean tests using the CCF values of standardized residuals instead of squared standardized residuals, as is carried out in subsequent analyses in this chapter.

4.3. Data

We obtain daily data on 10-year Maastricht convergence bond yields from Eurostat, which are widely used for comparative studies of long-term sovereign bonds in Eurozone countries[4]. With regard to banking sector equities in the four investigated countries, we extract daily values on the DataStream stock market indices in the banking sector of each country from Thomson Financial DataStream. We focus on the banking sector partly because banks and financial institutions are considered to have been badly affected by the Greek sovereign debt crisis because of their direct holdings of Greek government bonds. Moreover, comparable datasets for the four countries studied over the test period are available only for the banking sector and not for other sub-sectors such as insurance and real estate.

The sample covers the period from 2 January 2007 to 30 June 2011. We divide the period into two sub-periods: the pre-crisis period (from 2 January 2007 to 4 November 2009) and the crisis period (from 5 November 2009 to 30 June 2011). We choose 5 November 2009 as the beginning of the debt crisis period because that was when the Greek government disclosed that its fiscal deficit was twice as much as it had announced previously[5]. This disclosure led market participants to realize that the nation faced a serious solvency issue.

We use daily data in our study for two primary reasons. First, we try to avoid the issue of aggregation effects, which using less frequent data may trigger. Second, daily datasets contain a sufficient number of samples to enable us to analyse the impacts of relatively recent events, such as the Greek sovereign debt crisis.

Table 4.1 summarizes the descriptive statistics of the data on Greek long-term sovereign bond yields and southern European banking sector stock indices. The mean of the Greek bond yield returns increased (i.e. the interest rates soared) during the course of the crisis, but the mean of the stock index returns decreased, except in Italy. With regard to the movement in volatilities, the standard deviation of Greek bond yields, Greek stock indices, and Portuguese stock indices increased, whereas that of the stock indices of other countries decreased. Further, the Jarque–Bera tests rejected normality for all cases, regardless of the sub-sample periods.

By employing an ADF test, we identified the unit root processes for level data, but not for the first log-differenced data of government bond yields and banking sector stocks at the 1% significance level, as shown in Table 4.2. Hence, we express the data as percentage changes over the previous period, as is common in existing literature.

4.4.   Empirical results

Table 4.3 summarizes the parameter estimates for each of the selected AR(k)-EGARCH(p,q) models. The lag lengths in the return equations differ across each time series in each sub-sample period. However, we select the EGARCH(1,1) model for all the time series in the variance equations. It is noticeable that all the coefficients of the ARCH(α_i), GARCH(β_i), and asymmetric (γ_i) terms are statistically significant at the 5% level, with the exception of the ARCH term of the Greek banking sector stock indices during the crisis period. Here, $Q(20)$ and $Q^2(20)$ represent the Ljung–Box statistics used to test for the null hypothesis of no autocorrelation up to order 20 for the standard residuals and standard residuals squared, respectively. As indicated in Table 4.3, both statistics are well above 0.05 in all cases. Hence, the null hypothesis of no autocorrelation up to order 20 for the standardized residuals and standardized residuals squared is accepted at the 5% significance level. These results empirically support our specification of the presented AR-EGARCH models[6].

Tables 4.4, 4.5, 4.6, and 4.7 report Hong's (2001) Q-statistics used to test for the null hypothesis of no causality up to lag M ($= 5$, 10, 15), measured in days,

Table 4.1 Summary of statistics

	GR Sovereign Bond	GR Banking Stock	PT Banking Stock	IT Banking Stock	ES Banking Stock
Entire sample (2 January 2007–30 June 2011)					
Mean (percentage)	0.12	−0.17	−0.13	−0.10	−0.06
Median (percentage)	0.00	−0.01	−0.04	−0.05	−0.02
Maximum (percentage)	11.51	12.98	12.79	15.79	19.06
Minimum (percentage)	−11.91	−11.10	−10.10	−9.90	−11.51
SD (percentage)	1.68	2.83	1.89	2.23	2.31
Skewness	0.22	0.28	0.20	0.25	0.56
Kurtosis	13.14	5.08	7.19	8.37	10.06
Jarque–Bera	5031.4***	227.4***	865.5***	1419.9***	2491.1***
Pre-crisis period (2 January 2007–4 November 2009)					
Mean (percentage)	0.02	−0.09	−0.11	−0.11	−0.05
Median (percentage)	0.00	0.13	0.00	−0.01	−0.03
Maximum (percentage)	5.82	11.60	9.09	10.96	12.04
Minimum (percentage)	−4.69	−11.10	−10.10	−9.90	−11.51
SD (percentage)	1.10	2.57	1.86	2.30	2.33
Skewness	0.53	0.05	−0.01	−0.01	0.17
Kurtosis	5.96	5.87	6.66	7.28	7.35
Jarque–Bera	304.5***	254.8***	414.0***	567.3***	588.9***
Crisis period (5 November 2009–30 June 2011)					
Mean (percentage)	0.29	−0.31	−0.16	−0.10	−0.08
Median (percentage)	0.13	−0.44	−0.15	−0.14	−0.02
Maximum (percentage)	11.51	12.98	12.79	15.79	19.06
Minimum (percentage)	−11.91	−10.22	−7.06	−7.20	−8.69
SD (percentage)	2.36	3.22	1.95	2.10	2.29
Skewness	−0.04	0.53	0.53	0.85	1.27
Kurtosis	8.76	4.21	7.95	10.85	15.15
Jarque–Bera	592.4***	46.4***	458.6***	1152.6***	2752.4***

Notes: Statistics for the log-differences on the daily bond yields and daily stock prices multiplied by 100 are reported.

Countries are abbreviated as follows: GR (Greece), PT (Portugal), IT (Italy), and ES (Spain).

*** denotes statistical significance at the 1% level.

Table 4.2 Results of ADF unit root tests

	GR Sovereign Bond	GR Banking Stock	PT Banking Stock	IT Banking Stock	ES Banking Stock
Entire sample (2 January 2007–30 June 2011)					
Without time trend (1% critical value = −3.44)					
ADF test statistic	−30.70	−32.35	−31.07	−32.19	−32.66
p-value	0.0000	0.0000	0.0000	0.0000	0.0000
With time trend (1% critical value = −3.97)					
ADF test statistic	−30.76	−32.34	−31.06	−32.18	−32.65
p-value	0.0000	0.0000	0.0000	0.0000	0.0000
Pre-crisis period (2 January 2007–4 November 2009)					
Without time trend (1% critical value = −3.44)					
ADF test statistic	−24.20	−24.62	−24.94	−13.17	−26.51
p-value	0.0000	0.0000	0.0000	0.0000	0.0000
With time trend (1% critical value = −3.97)					
ADF test statistic	−24.21	−24.61	−24.93	−13.17	−26.52
p-value	0.0000	0.0000	0.0000	0.0000	0.0000
Crisis period (5 November 2009–30 June 2011)					
Without time trend (1% critical value = −3.45)					
ADF test statistic	−18.74	−20.58	−15.49	−19.66	−19.03
p-value	0.0000	0.0000	0.0000	0.0000	0.0000
With time trend (1% critical value = −3.98)					
ADF test statistic	−18.73	−20.59	−15.47	−19.64	−19.01
p-value	0.0000	0.0000	0.0000	0.0000	0.0000

Notes: The unit root processes for the first log-differenced data are analysed above.

Countries are abbreviated as follows: GR (Greece), PT (Portugal), IT (Italy), and ES (Spain).

for each combination of Greek long-term bond yields and the banking sector stock indices of the four investigated countries, before and during the Greek sovereign debt crisis. Figure 4.1 graphically indicates the detected causality-in-mean and causality-in-variance. From these results, we extract three interesting findings.

First, we find support for the significant causality-in-mean effects seen from bank stock returns in Greece to Greek long-term bond yields – but only during the sovereign debt crisis period. In contrast, the reverse causality (i.e. the negative

Table 4.3 Results of AR-EGARCH models

Pre-crisis period (2 January 2007–4 November 2009)

	GR Sovereign Bond AR(4)–GARCH(1,1)		GR Banking Stock AR(10)–EGARCH(1,1)		PT Banking Stock AR(10)–EGARCH(1,1)		IT Banking Stock AR(10)–EGARCH(1,1)		ES Banking Stock AR(10)–EGARCH(1,1)	
	Estimate	SE	Estimate	SE	Estimate	SE	Estimate	SE	Estimate	SE
Return equation										
a_0	0.013	0.040	−0.043	0.068	0.011	0.051	−0.122**	0.058	−0.105	0.060
a_1	0.080	0.043	0.068	0.045	0.086**	0.038	0.038	0.043	0.026	0.042
a_2	0.099**	0.040	0.005	0.036	0.020	0.039	0.014	0.040	−0.003	0.038
a_3	0.026	0.036	0.012	0.042	0.035	0.039	−0.009	0.039	0.053	0.038
a_4	−0.061	0.039	0.066	0.037	0.042	0.039	0.039	0.036	0.021	0.036
a_5			−0.061	0.041	0.004	0.037	−0.068	0.037	−0.020	0.037
a_6			−0.093***	0.036	−0.026	0.037	0.020	0.037	−0.005	0.035
a_7			−0.001	0.039	0.054	0.040	−0.022	0.040	−0.016	0.035
a_8			−0.037	0.041	0.015	0.041	0.049	0.039	0.077**	0.032
a_9			0.012	0.037	−0.023	0.039	0.054	0.037	0.069	0.037
a_{10}			0.040	0.037	0.061	0.041	0.051	0.038	0.064	0.034
Variance equation										
ω	−0.146***	0.030	−0.114***	0.020	−0.114***	0.025	−0.061***	0.017	−0.098***	0.027
α_1	0.233***	0.043	0.199***	0.032	0.199***	0.033	0.109***	0.024	0.160***	0.036
γ_1	0.059**	0.029	−0.069***	0.019	−0.097***	0.020	−0.087***	0.015	−0.178***	0.027
β_1	0.775***	0.059	0.979***	0.005	0.964***	0.008	0.985***	0.003	0.983***	0.005
Log-likelihood	−1089.6		−1600.7		−1397.8		−1476.3		−1474.2	
$Q(20)$	13.750		12.780		7.702		14.017		21.276	
p-value	0.843		0.887		0.994		0.830		0.381	
$Q(20)$	21.274		17.061		23.021		12.136		22.144	
p-value	0.381		0.649		0.288		0.911		0.333	

(Continued)

Table 4.3 (Continued)

Crisis period (5 November 2009–30 June 2011)

	GR Sovereign Bond AR(3)–GARCH(1,1)		GR Banking Stock AR(1)–EGARCH(1,1)		PT Banking Stock AR(10)–EGARCH(1,1)		IT Banking Stock AR(10)–EGARCH(1,1)		ES Banking Stock AR(10)–EGARCH(1,1)	
	Estimate	SE	Estimate	SE	Estimate	SE	Estimate	SE	Estimate	SE
Return equation										
α_0	0.177	0.103	-0.376**	0.160	-0.146	0.086	-0.172	0.091	-0.181**	0.091
α_1	0.176***	0.065	0.016	0.053	0.125**	0.050	0.066	0.059	0.076	0.052
α_2	0.091	0.052			-0.080	0.054	-0.090	0.051	-0.089	0.056
α_3	-0.076	0.072			-0.046	0.051	0.044	0.055	0.055	0.050
α_4					0.000	0.052	-0.046	0.045	-0.045	0.044
α_5					0.014	0.053	0.065	0.053	-0.007	0.048
α_6					0.061	0.053	-0.050	0.048	-0.026	0.049
α_7					0.033	0.052	0.062	0.047	0.045	0.045
α_8					-0.104**	0.051	-0.035	0.050	-0.085	0.052
α_9					-0.049	0.052	0.036	0.045	0.027	0.048
α_{10}					-0.003	0.054	-0.043	0.054	-0.066	0.050
Variance equation										
ω	-0.052**	0.025	0.277	0.170	-0.059	0.042	-0.032	0.044	-0.106**	0.046
α_1	0.249***	0.044	0.093	0.055	0.165***	0.056	0.144***	0.054	0.237***	0.057
γ_1	0.075**	0.032	-0.114**	0.046	-0.125***	0.037	-0.177***	0.035	-0.210***	0.044
β_1	0.923***	0.011	0.850***	0.079	0.939***	0.028	0.941***	0.026	0.947***	0.023
Log-likelihood	-937.0		-1098.0		-829.2		-862.7		-879.0	
Q(20)	21.304		19.696		11.309		12.943		12.100	
p-value	0.379		0.477		0.938		0.880		0.913	
Q^2(20)	8.335		17.151		13.201		23.348		24.046	
p-value	0.989		0.643		0.869		0.272		0.240	

Notes: $Q(20)$ and $Q^2(20)$ are the Ljung–Box statistics up to the 20th orders in standardized residuals and standardized residuals squared, respectively. Countries are abbreviated as follows: GR (Greece), PT (Portugal), IT (Italy), and ES (Spain).

*** and ** denote statistical significance at the 1% and 5% levels, respectively.

impact of interest rate changes on the country's bank stock returns) is nonsignificant. One possible reason for the detected causality from bank stock returns to bond yield changes is that, in the short run, the crisis may have strengthened the forward-looking nature of stock returns in troubled banking sectors. As Alaganar and Bhar (2003) contend, banking sector stock prices can incorporate the expectations of market participants on the state of the economy and on future interest rates.

Second, we find evidence of significant causality at the mean level from bank stock returns in Portugal, Italy, and Spain to Greek sovereign bond yields. This causality is transient up to lag 5 and prevalent both before and during the crisis period in Portugal but only during the crisis period in Italy. One reason behind this causality is that market participants believe that Greece's solvency depends on its chances of being bailed out by its neighbouring nations. Thus, any slump in the bank stock returns in those countries may affect Greek bond yields. This finding implies that the short-term relationship between Greek bond yields and southern European bank stock returns is more intricate than the one-way causality from interest rates to stock prices, which most previous studies have tended to assume when examining these relations over longer horizons.

Third, we detect bidirectional causality-in-variance from and to Greek long-term bond yields, which emerged after the crisis, in banking sector stocks in

Table 4.4 Cross correlation analysis between Greek bond yields and Greek banking stock indices

	Causality-in-Mean		Causality-in-Variance	
M	*GRBK→GRB*	*GRB→GRBK*	*GRBK→GRB*	*GRB→GRBK*
Pre-crisis period (2 January 2007–4 November 2009)				
5	0.99	−0.84	1.04	0.48
10	0.30	−1.59	0.98	0.34
15	−0.02	−1.16	0.57	0.21
Crisis period (5 November 2009–30 June 2011)				
5	3.70***	−0.74	0.11	−1.17
10	3.43***	−0.97	−0.39	−1.44
15	3.50***	−0.43	−0.99	−1.51

Notes: Table entries indicate values of the Q-statistic based on the Hong (2001) approach.

The Q-statistic is used to test the null hypothesis of no-causality from lag 1 up to lag M ($M = 5, 10, 15$).

The Q-statistic is based on one-side tests. Lags are measured in days.

Each asset is abbreviated as follows: GRB (Greek sovereign bond) and GRBK (Greek banking sector stock).

*** denotes statistical significance at the 1% level.

Table 4.5 Cross correlation analysis between Greek bond yields and Portuguese banking stock indices

M	Causality-in-Mean		Causality-in-Variance	
	PTBK→GRB	GRB→PTBK	PTBK→GRB	GRB→PTBK
Pre-crisis period (2 January 2007–4 November 2009)				
5	1.96**	−0.16	4.98***	−0.49
10	0.79	−0.15	2.87***	−0.92
15	0.04	0.81	3.56***	0.72
Crisis period (5 November 2009–30 June 2011)				
5	2.65***	0.58	2.46***	1.93**
10	1.15	0.00	1.40	1.11
15	0.99	−0.52	1.09	0.39

Notes: Table entries indicate values of the Q-statistic based on the Hong (2001) approach.

The Q-statistic is used to test the null hypothesis of no-causality from lag 1 up to lag M (M = 5, 10, 15).

The Q-statistic is based on one-side tests. Lags are measured in days.

Each asset is abbreviated as follows: GRB (Greek sovereign bond) and PTBK (Portuguese banking sector stock).

*** and ** denote statistical significance at the 1% and 5% levels, respectively.

Table 4.6 Cross correlation analysis between Greek bond yields and Italian banking stock indices

M	Causality-in-Mean		Causality-in-Variance	
	ITBK→GRB	GRB→ITBK	ITBK→GRB	GRB→ITBK
Pre-crisis period (2 January 2007–4 November 2009)				
5	1.18	0.39	1.73**	0.37
10	0.05	−0.40	2.02**	1.48
15	−0.43	−0.20	3.95***	1.06
Crisis period (5 November 2009–30 June 2011)				
5	2.69***	−0.73	1.90**	−0.04
10	1.69**	−0.92	1.58	2.38***
15	1.06	−0.82	0.96	2.82***

Notes: Table entries indicate values of the Q-statistic based on the Hong (2001) approach.

The Q-statistic is used to test the null hypothesis of no-causality from lag 1 up to lag M (M = 5, 10, 15).

The Q-statistic is based on one-side tests. Lags are measured in days.

Each asset is abbreviated as follows: GRB (Greek sovereign bond) and ITBK (Italian banking sector stock).

*** and ** denote statistical significance at the 1% and 5% levels, respectively.

Table 4.7 Cross correlation analysis between Greek bond yields and Spanish banking stock indices

M	Causality-in-Mean		Causality-in-Variance	
	ESBK→GRB	GRB→ESBK	ESBK→GRB	GRB→ESBK
Pre-crisis period (2 January 2007–4 November 2009)				
5	2.42***	0.06	1.37	0.59
10	0.61	−0.49	0.70	0.66
15	−0.29	0.45	2.11**	0.75
Crisis period (5 November 2009–30 June 2011)				
5	1.67**	−0.56	2.02**	−0.10
10	0.72	−0.85	2.00**	2.03**
15	0.13	−1.39	0.95	1.50

Notes: Table entries indicate values of the Q-statistic based on the Hong (2001) approach.

The Q-statistic is used to test the null hypothesis of no-causality from lag 1 up to lag M ($M = 5, 10, 15$).

The Q-statistic is based on one-side tests. Lags are measured in days.

Each asset is abbreviated as follows: GRB (Greek sovereign bond) and ESBK (Spanish banking sector stock).

*** and ** denote statistical significance at the 1% and 5% levels, respectively.

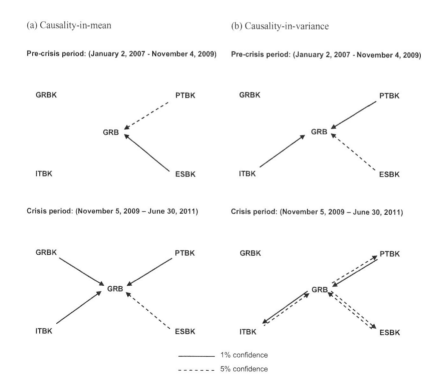

Figure 4.1 Causality-in-mean and causality-in-variance by Q-tests from lag 1 up to lag M ($M = 5, 10,$ or 15)

Portugal, Italy, and Spain. This finding of a two-way causal linkage is consistent with those of Alaganar and Bhar (2003). The emerging volatility spillovers from Greek bond yields to banking sector equity returns may indicate that the banking sectors of Portugal, Italy, and Spain were vulnerable to the solvency risks of the Greek sovereign bonds they held. As the onset of the debt crisis made market participants fully realize the risks, the volatilities may have begun to reflect these information flows significantly, even though they were not captured in the causality at the mean level. Nonetheless, we should also mention that the sovereign debt crisis may have affected all four countries at the same time and that a common factor may have driven this apparent bidirectional causality during the crisis period. If this were the case, the detected causality would be considered spurious. Thus, investigating the existence of such a common factor would call for different methodologies, because Hong's (2001) approach focuses on testing the short-term dynamics between only two variables.

4.5. Conclusion

This study investigated the causality-in-variance and causality-in-mean between Greek long-term bond yields and the banking sector equity returns of four southern European countries based on daily data from January 2007 to June 2011. It focused on assessing the potential impacts of the recent European sovereign debt crisis. To conduct the causality tests, we used the robust CCF approach developed by Hong (2001), which does not rely on simultaneous inter-series modelling and, thereby, allows for flexible specifications of innovation processes.

The main findings from our analysis are threefold. First, the significant unidirectional causality-in-mean from bank stock returns in Greece to Greek long-term bond yields arises only during the sovereign debt crisis period. Second, we also detect significant causality-in-mean from the bank equity returns in Portugal, Italy, and Spain to Greek sovereign bond yields. Third, and most interestingly, we find significant evidence of bidirectional causality-in-variance between Greek long-term bond yields and the banking sector stocks in Portugal, Italy, and Spain during the debt crisis. Thus, the presented empirical results are relevant to regulators of the banking sectors in the investigated countries, as well as bank managers in the affected countries. Specifically, our empirical results highlight the importance of closely monitoring potential volatility spillovers from soaring sovereign risks of one country, as reflected in its government bond yields, to the banking sector stock index returns of neighbouring nations, and avoiding the adverse effects of the spillovers.

The present study also considered the possibility that Greek bond yields influence the banking stock returns in neighbouring nations by affecting the bond markets in these countries. Although this study focused on examining the relationship between the Greek bond market, the origin of the crisis, and southern European bank equity markets, future studies should consider analysing the causalities among sovereign bond yields in different markets.

Notes

1 See Nelson (1991) for details of the EGARCH model.
2 Hong's (2001) approach is typically used in a bivariate framework because it allows dealing with two variables at once. Some previous studies have conducted Granger causality tests with multiple variables as a system. For instance, Lee (1992), using a vector autoregression (VAR) system, investigates the relationships among stock returns, interest rates, inflation rates, and growth in industrial production. Our study focuses specifically on the bivariate relationship between bank stock returns and bond yields.
3 In terms of the weighting function, $k(z)$, we select the truncated kernel, which provides compact support. By performing Monte Carlo experiments, Hong (2001) contends that for a smaller M (i.e. $M = 10$), the truncated kernel gives approximately similar power to non-uniform kernels, such as the Bartlett, Daniell, and QS kernels. For the application of the Hong test, refer to, for example, Xu and Hamori (2012) and Tamakoshi and Hamori (2013).
4 One possible choice for the Greek government bond data is to use the risk premium on bond prices, because we use stock price-level data to represent the banking sector. Nevertheless, we employ bond yields data to ensure that the results of our analysis are comparable to those of similar studies, such as Alaganar and Bhar (2003).
5 We selected this date based on the key event that signified the onset of the crisis, as is common in related literature. Nonetheless, we also need to mention that the break date in the time series could be earlier or later than this announcement by the Greek government. Indeed, some methodologies detect structural breakpoints endogenously, although these statistical procedures do have their own limitations. For instance, Bai and Perron (1998, 2003) describe how to estimate the location of multiple endogenous structural breaks in mean and variance parameters.
6 However, note that even though the variance equation in the pre-crisis period displays a very good fit to the EGARCH specification, the fit of the equation in the crisis period is relatively poor. An alternative approach that may be useful for considering the effect of the crisis in the EGARCH framework, although not used in this study, is to include a dummy variable in the conditional variance equation.

References

Alaganar, V., Bhar, R. (2003) An international study of causality-in-variance: Interest rate and financial sector returns, *Journal of Economics and Finance*, **27**, 39–54.

Bae, S.C. (1990) Interest rate changes and common stock returns of financial institutions: Revisited, *Journal of Financial Research*, **13**, 71–79.

Bai, J., Perron, P. (1998) Estimating and testing linear models with multiple structural changes, *Econometrica*, **66**, 47–78.

Bai, J., Perron, P. (2003) Computation and analysis of multiple structural change models, *Journal of Applied Econometrics*, **18**, 1–22.

Bollerslev, T. (1986) Generalized autoregressive conditional heteroskedasticity, *Journal of Econometrics*, **52**, 5–59.

Chance, D.M., Lane, W.R. (1980) A re-examination of interest rate sensitivity in the common stocks of financial institutions, *Journal of Financial Research*, **3**, 49–55.

Cheung, Y., Ng, L. (1996) A causality-in-variance test and its applications to financial market prices, *Journal of Econometrics*, **72**, 33–48.

Elyasiani, E., Mansur, I. (1998) Sensitivity of the bank distribution to changes in the level and volatility of interest rate: A GARCH-M model, *Journal of Banking & Finance*, **22**, 535–563.

Elyasiani, E., Mansur, I. (2004) Bank stock return sensitivities to the long-term and short-term interest rates: A multivariate GARCH approach, *Managerial Finance*, **30**, 32–55.

Engle, R.F. (1982) Autoregressive conditional heteroskedasticity with estimates of the variance of United Kingdom inflation, *Econometrica*, **50**, 987–1007.

Engle, R.F., Ito, T., Lin, K.L. (1990) Meteor showers or heat waves? Heteroskedastic intra-daily volatility in the foreign exchange market, *Econometrica*, **58**, 525–542.

Flannery, M.J., James, C.M. (1984) The effect of interest rate changes on the common stock returns of financial institutions, *Journal of Finance*, **39**, 1141–1153.

Hong, Y. (2001) A test for volatility spillover with application to exchange rates, *Journal of Econometrics*, **103**, 183–224.

Lee, B.S. (1992) Causal relations among stock returns, interest rates, real activity, and inflation, *Journal of Finance*, **47**, 1591–1603.

Lloyd, W.P., Shick, R.A. (1977) A test of Stone's two-index model of returns, *Journal of Financial and Quantitative Analysis*, **12**, 363–376.

Nelson, D. (1991) Conditional heteroskedasticity in asset returns: A new approach, *Econometrica*, **59**, 347–370.

Ross, S.A. (1989) Information and volatility: No-arbitrage Martingale approach to timing and resolution irrelevancy, *Journal of Finance*, **44**, 1–17.

Shiller, R.J., Beltratti, A.E. (1992) Can their co-movements be explained in terms of present value models? *Journal of Monetary Economics*, **30**, 25–46.

Song, F. (1994) A two-factor ARCH model for deposit-institution stock returns, *Journal of Money, Credit, and Banking*, **26**, 323–340.

Tai, C.S. (2000) Time-varying market, interest rate, and exchange rate risk premia in the U.S. commercial bank stock returns, *Journal of Multinational Finance Management*, **10**, 397–420.

Tamakoshi, G., Hamori, S. (2013) Volatility and mean spillovers between sovereign and banking sector CDS markets: A note on the European sovereign debt crisis, *Applied Economics Letters*, **20**, 262–266.

Verma, P., Jackson, O.D. (2008) Interest rate and bank stock returns asymmetry: Evidence from U.S. banks, *Journal of Economics and Finance*, **32**, 105–118.

Xu, H., Hamori, S. (2012) Dynamic linkages of stock prices between the BRICs and the United States: Effects of the 2008–09 financial crisis, *Journal of Asian Economics*, **23**, 344–352.

5 Causality between the US dollar and the euro LIBOR-OIS spreads

5.1. Introduction

Since August 2007, the money markets in the US and the euro area have experienced turbulence, with unprecedentedly high short-term funding costs. This led to both practitioners and academics paying close attention to one particular measure of stress in interbank money markets: the LIBOR-OIS spread, defined as the difference between the London Interbank Offer Rate (LIBOR)[1] and the overnight index swap (OIS)[2]. For example, the 3-month LIBOR-OIS spread was under 10 basis points in early August 2007 but rose sharply to almost 400 basis points right after the failure of Lehman Brothers in September 2008, although the central banks intervened by temporarily increasing the supply of liquidity.

Academic studies have triggered debates on whether the LIBOR-OIS spread measures the system's liquidity stress or credit pressure. For instance, Michaud and Upper (2008) and Kwan (2009) argue that the widening LIBOR-OIS spread since August 2007 is better explained by changes in liquidity factors, rather than credit risk premium. In contrast, Taylor and Williams (2008) support its classification as a measurement of credit risk, reasoning that increasing counter-party risks among banks leads to increases in the spread. Such mixed results can be attributed to the difficulty in gauging liquidity stress explicitly. These prior studies indicate that the LIBOR-OIS spread could measure both liquidity and credit stress in the interbank market.

Another line of research in the existing literature focuses on assessing cross-currency causality in the LIBOR-OIS currency spreads. Using a standard vector autoregression (VAR) model, Imakubo et al. (2008) uncover the significant causality running from the US dollar (USD) LIBOR spread to the euro (EUR) and the Japanese yen (JPY) LIBOR spreads during the period of the global financial crisis. Ji and In (2010) employ a more formal VAR model and an impulse response function analysis, based on bias-corrected bootstrap methods, and detect that the crisis increased the persistence of shocks of the USD spread in the response functions of other currency LIBOR spreads. The present chapter follows this strand of research; however, unlike prior studies, which focus solely on analysing mean transmission effects, it examines the causality-in-variance between the USD and the EUR LIBOR-OIS spreads in a cross-currency framework for the first time.

One of the main motivations for our analysis stems from the importance of clarifying the difference between the causality-in-mean and causality-in-variance. It is understood that the causality-in-mean effect can be explained by the wealth effect, as noted by Kyle and Xiong (2001). According to their study, the wealth effect emerges when rational traders, who are pursuing short-term profit-making opportunities by taking the opposite side of noise traders, face substantial losses and thereby need to liquidate their positions. In such cases, the reduced liquidity in both markets makes the asset returns more volatile and more correlated, resulting in a causality-in-mean. In contrast, Ross (1989), who shows that volatility is related to the extent to which market participants assimilate information, utilises the causality-in-variance effect. From this perspective, causality-in-variance is concerned with transmission of information across different markets. Engle et al. (1990) call the volatility spillover effects from one market to another 'the meteor showers'. Furthermore, some authors note that the existence of volatility spillovers is consistent with a failure of the strong form market efficiency. For example, Kyle (1985) develops a model where volatility spillover is triggered when information is gradually processed and thus is fully incorporated into the price only at the end of the trading interval. In this context, the causality-in-variance is associated with the speed of market adjustment to information.

We examine the volatility and mean spillovers using the CCF approach developed by Hong (2001). There are several advantages of employing the CCF approach. The test makes no distributional assumptions and exhibits greater power than conventional Granger causality tests. In addition, since the test does not require simultaneous modelling, its implementation is less complex than that of a multivariate general autoregressive conditional heteroskedasticity (GARCH) framework. Moreover, the test can detect the persistence of causality. The CCF method developed by Hong (2001) overcomes the key weakness of the Cheung and Ng (1996) approach that relies on a counter-intuitive assumption of weighting each lag uniformly.

Using daily data covering a longer period than those in prior studies, we examine the impacts of not only the 2007–2009 global financial crisis but also the recent European sovereign debt crisis on the bivariate relationships between the USD and EUR LIBOR-OIS spreads. As the recent debt crisis is believed to have worsened the counterparty risks of the European financial institutions holding large amounts of Greek government debt, it is worthwhile to examine how the crisis affected the LIBOR-OIS spreads, which partially gauge credit risks. The knowledge of the direction and timing of the transmission of information among the LIBOR-OIS spreads, manifested through our analysis, will help policymakers gauge the efficiency of the money market and whether they should intervene under market strains.

The remainder of this chapter is organized as follows. Section 5.2 explains our dataset and Section 5.3 reports the empirical results. Finally, concluding remarks are presented in Section 5.4.

5.2. Data

Our data utilises 1,693 daily observations of LIBOR-OIS spreads, covering the period from January 2005 to June 2011. The beginning of the period is constrained by availability of data, which was extracted from Datastream. Following Imakubo et al. (2008) and Ji and In (2010), we use the 3-month LIBOR-OIS spreads for both the USD and EUR, computed as the difference between their respective LIBOR and OIS rates. The entire sample is divided into three sub-periods: the pre-crisis period (Panel A; from 4 January 2005 to 8 August 2007), the global financial crisis period (Panel B; from 9 August 2007 to 15 December 2009), and the European sovereign debt crisis period (Panel C; from 16 December 2009 to 30 June 2011). Similar to the previous literature, we select 9 August 2007 as the commencement of the global financial crisis period because on that day, BNP Paribas acknowledged the impact of the crisis by closing two mutual funds exposed to subprime loan liabilities. With regard to the onset of the European debt crisis, we choose 16 December 2009, when Standard & Poor's lowered the sovereign credit rating of Greece from A1 to BBB+, triggering concerns over the country's solvency. Both of these events caused the 3-month LIBOR-OIS spreads to increase abruptly.

Figure 5.1 plots the historical values of the 3-month USD and EUR LIBOR-OIS spreads. Both the spreads were close to zero prior to August 2007 but rose to over 350 basis points and stayed high until October 2009. Table 5.1 provides some descriptive statistics for the first-differenced data of our dataset. Note that both spreads exhibit high standard deviations, especially during the period of

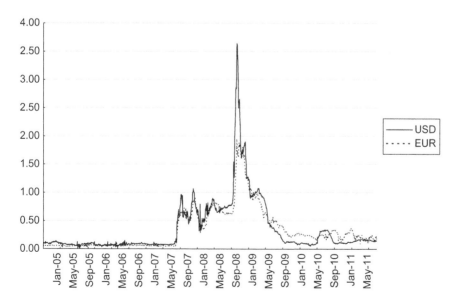

Figure 5.1 3-month LIBOR-OIS spreads in US dollars (USD) and euro (EUR) (in percentage)

Table 5.1 Summary of statistics

Variable	Mean	Max	Min	SD	Skewness	Kurtosis	Jarque–Bera
Entire sample							
USD	0.00003	0.391	−0.365	0.038	0.808	40.621	100,022.000***
EUR	0.00007	0.290	−0.155	0.024	1.338	25.048	34,797.000***
Panel A: Pre-crisis period							
USD	0.00006	0.091	−0.079	0.014	0.161	13.63	3,189.881***
EUR	0.00008	0.091	−0.083	0.011	0.372	20.703	8,856.252***
Panel B: Global financial crisis period							
USD	−0.00011	0.391	−0.365	0.062	0.534	16.605	4,764.588***
EUR	0.00026	0.290	−0.155	0.034	1.275	14.887	3,781.381***
Panel C: European sovereign debt crisis period							
USD	0.00018	0.080	−0.024	0.007	3.494	41.820	26,059.710***
EUR	−0.00025	0.096	−0.121	0.020	−0.556	11.839	1,329.255***

Notes: Statistics for first-differenced data are reported. The entire sample period was divided into Panel A (from 4 January 2005 to 8 August 2007), Panel B (from 9 August 2007 to 15 December 2009), and Panel C (from 16 December 2009 to 30 June 2011).

*** denotes statistical significance at the 1% level.

Table 5.2 Unit root tests: ADF

	USD		EUR	
	Trend	No trend	Trend	No trend
Level	−2.243	−2.277	−2.169	−2.216
First differences	−10.644***	−10.637***	−7.756***	−7.742***

*** denotes statistical significance at the 1% level. Critical values are based on MacKinnon (1991).

the global financial crisis. In addition, the high kurtosis statistics indicate that extreme changes in the spreads tend to occur frequently. The Jarque–Bera test rejects normality for all series, regardless of the sub-sample periods. Table 5.2 indicates the results of the ADF unit root test. We find that both the USD and EUR spreads are I (1) variables. Thus, we use first-differenced data in our subsequent analysis, which is common in literature on LIBOR-OIS spreads.

5.3.   Empirical results

As explained above, we employ the CCF methodology of Hong (2001), which consists of the following two steps. Our first step is to fit a univariate model to each data series. We choose the best of AR(k)-EGARCH(p, q) models, given as follows:[3]

$$\Delta y_t = \phi_0 + \sum\nolimits_{i=1}^{k} \phi_i \Delta y_{t-1} + \varepsilon_t, \quad z_t = \varepsilon_t / \sigma_t, \quad z_t \sim GED(v) \text{ and} \tag{1}$$

$$\log(\sigma_t^2) = \omega + \sum\nolimits_{i=1}^{q} (\alpha_i |z_{t-i}| + \gamma_i z_{t-i}) + \sum\nolimits_{i=1}^{p} \beta_i \log(\sigma_{t-i}^2), \tag{2}$$

where Δy_t represents the first difference of each time series, and ε_t is the error term, with $E_{t-1}(\varepsilon_t) = 0$ and $E_{t-1}(\varepsilon_t^2) = \sigma_t^2$. We assume that a random variable z_t has a generalized error distribution (GED). We select k ($= 1, 2, \ldots, 10$), p ($= 1, 2$), and q ($= 1, 2$) based on the Schwarz Bayesian Information Criterion (SBIC) and residual diagnostics on autocorrelation. The logarithm form of the EGARCH model ensures non-negativity of the conditional variance, and hence it is not constrained by the signs of the coefficients. The coefficients of the ARCH terms can capture asymmetric effects of both positive and negative shocks.

Table 5.3 reports the estimates of coefficients for each of the selected AR (k) – EGARCH (p, q) models. Our information criterion selects the EGARCH (1, 1)

Table 5.3 Results of AR-EGARCH models

Panel A: Pre-crisis period

	USD		EUR	
	AR(3)−EGARCH(1,1)		AR(4)−EGARCH(1,1)	
	Estimate	*SE*	*Estimate*	*SE*
Return equation				
ϕ_0	−0.00030	0.00015	−0.00011	0.00016
ϕ_1	−0.372***	0.029	−0.490***	0.032
ϕ_2	−0.232***	0.029	−0.264***	0.036
ϕ_3	−0.103***	0.026	−0.101***	0.034
ϕ_4			−0.074***	0.029
ϕ_5				
Variance equation				
ω	−1.324***	0.275	−0.563***	0.168
α_1	0.566***	0.091	0.304***	0.065
γ_1	−0.055	0.065	0.001	0.051
β_1	0.899***	0.026	0.964***	0.014
GED parameter	0.841***	0.048	0.991***	0.058
$Q(20)$	14.331		28.378	
p-value	0.813		0.101	
$Q^2(20)$	5.090		22.539	
p-value	1.000		0.312	

(*Continued*)

Table 5.3 (Continued)

Panel B: Global financial crisis period

	USD		EUR	
	AR(4)–EGARCH(1,1)		AR(5)–EGARCH(1,1)	
	Estimate	SE	Estimate	SE
Return equation				
ϕ_0	−0.00114***	0.00044	−0.00090**	0.00042
ϕ_1	0.128***	0.036	0.053**	0.027
ϕ_2	0.164***	0.035	0.027	0.024
ϕ_3	0.037	0.033	0.052**	0.021
ϕ_4	0.066**	0.031	0.054***	0.020
ϕ_5			0.086***	0.023
Variance equation				
ω	−0.500***	0.087	−0.516***	0.152
α_1	0.482***	0.061	0.329***	0.063
γ_1	0.070	0.043	0.057	0.044
β_1	0.979***	0.010	0.960***	0.017
GED parameter	0.995***	0.067	0.806***	0.054
$Q(20)$	27.583		18.279	
p-value	0.120		0.569	
$Q^2(20)$	18.166		8.888	
p-value	0.576		0.984	

Panel C: European sovereign crisis period

	USD		EUR	
	AR(4)–EGARCH(1,1)		AR(1)–EGARCH(1,1)	
	Estimate	SE	Estimate	SE
Return equation				
ϕ_0	0.00005	0.00022	−0.00018	0.00032
ϕ_1	−0.057***	0.053	−0.079**	0.031
ϕ_2	0.134***	0.044		
ϕ_3	0.108***	0.042		
ϕ_4	0.177***	0.029		
ϕ_5				
Variance equation				
ω	−5.231***	1.682	−0.252**	0.100
α_1	0.652***	0.121	0.202***	0.061
γ_1	−0.050	0.089	−0.133***	0.051
β_1	0.543***	0.158	0.986***	0.011

(*Continued*)

Table 5.3 (Continued)

| | USD AR(4)–EGARCH(1,1) | | EUR AR(1)–EGARCH(1,1) | |
	Estimate	SE	Estimate	SE
GED parameter	1.182***	0.100	0.824***	0.062
$Q(20)$	26.778		20.409	
p-value	0.142		0.433	
$Q^2(20)$	17.442		2.656	
p-value	0.624		1.000	

Notes: $Q(20)$ and $Q^2(20)$ are the Ljung-Box statistics up to the 20th orders in standardized residuals and standardized residuals squared, respectively.

*** and ** denote statistical significance at the 1% and 5% levels, respectively.

model for all the series. In the variance equations, all the parameters, except for the asymmetric terms (γ_i) for most cases, are statistically significant at the 5% level. According to the Ljung-Box statistics $Q(20)$ and $Q^2(20)$, we accept the null hypothesis of no autocorrelation up to order 20 for the standard residuals and their squares. These results support the validity of our model specification.

Our second step is to use squared standardized residuals to conduct the causality-in-variance and causality-in-mean tests (we employ a similar process using the CCF of standardized residuals to test for causality-in-mean)[4]. In using the Hong (2001) Q-statistics, it is important to choose the weighting function $k(z)$ carefully, as it affects the statistical power of the test. We select the Barlett kernel, one of the non-uniform kernels that give superior power characteristics according to the Monte Carlo experiments in Hong (2001). The kernel is expressed as follows:

$$k(z) = \begin{cases} 1-|z|, & |z| \leq 1, \\ 0, & otherwise. \end{cases} \tag{3}$$

Table 5.4 reports the causality-in-mean and causality-in-variance test results up to M (= 5, 10, 15) lags, measured in days, for each pair of spreads. In summary, our key empirical findings are three-fold.

First, we find evidence of significant bi-directional causality-in-mean during the global financial crisis period but only significant causality from the USD to EUR up to 15 lags prior to the crisis. Based on the Q-statistic, we find the causality-in-mean effect from the USD to EUR to be more persistent than that in the opposite direction[5]. Such findings are generally in line with the results of Ji and In (2010), who investigate causality-in-mean using the impulse response analysis in a five-variable VAR system, with the USD placed first in the ordering. Our results confirm that the global financial crisis triggered liquidity tension in US dollar funding, as reflected in the widening USD LIBOR-OIS spreads, which resulted in higher stress on the EUR spreads, while generating feedback effects between the two.

Table 5.4 Hong (2001) cross-correlation analysis

Panel A: Pre-crisis period

	Causality-in-Mean		Causality-in-Variance	
M	EUR→USD	USD→EUR	EUR→USD	USD→EUR
5	−0.592	0.913	−1.008	0.422
10	−0.993	1.424	−1.462	0.526
15	−1.244	1.684**	−1.769	0.521

Panel B: Global financial crisis period

	Causality-in-Mean		Causality-in-Variance	
M	EUR→USD	USD→EUR	EUR→USD	USD→EUR
5	2.833***	2.213**	14.598***	0.376
10	3.890***	4.074***	15.550***	1.366
15	3.771**	4.815***	13.921***	1.366

Panel C: European sovereign debt crisis period

	Causality-in-Mean		Causality-in-Variance	
M	EUR→USD	USD→EUR	EUR→USD	USD→EUR
5	0.366	−1.078	0.197	−0.886
10	0.610	−1.446	0.309	−1.158
15	0.757	−1.551	0.078	−1.441

Notes: Table entries indicate values of the Q-statistic.

The Q-statistic is used to test the null hypothesis of no-causality from lag 1 up to lag M (M=5, 10, 15).

*** and ** indicate statistical significance at the 1% and 5% levels, respectively.

Second, we find significant unidirectional causality-in-variance from EUR to the USD emerging during the period of the global financial crisis. In contrast, the reverse causality from the USD to EUR is not significant during the crisis period. Note that causality-in-variance implies a pattern of transmission of volatility and indicates information flows, as Ross (1989) contends. One reason for the detected causality may be the changes in the funding behaviour of the euro-area financial institutions, which had substantial exposures to subprime-related products and probably faced heavy liquidity tensions. Imakubo et al. (2008) document that during the crisis period, the European banks obtained a large amount of US dollar funding from the FX swap markets in exchange for the euro. Such behaviour might have been accompanied by the widening of the EUR LIBOR-OIS spreads, resulting in significant causality from the EUR/USD FX swap markets to the USD interbank money market. The emerging transmissions of volatility from the EUR LIBOR-OIS spreads to the USD spreads during the crisis period may reflect such information flows.

Third, our results suggest that there are no significant causality-in-mean and causality-in-variance effects between the two spreads during the debt crisis period. This is interesting because it is widely believed that the debt crisis worsened the credit risks of financial institutions due to their large holdings of Greek sovereign bonds, and, hence, there is reason to believe that the LIBOR-OIS spreads reflect the surge of the banks' credit risks. On the one hand, finding no causality may only imply that the spreads better represent liquidity stress rather than credit risks in the context of cross-currency causality. Nevertheless, on the other hand, we consider that in May 2010, the European Central Bank announced the Securities Markets Programme, which was designed to purchase sovereign bonds in order to ensure liquidity and prevent potential spillovers from government bond markets to other markets. Moreover, additional liquidity measures such as the fixed-rate tender procedure with full allotment and the temporary liquidity swap lines with the Federal Reserve banks, which had been introduced earlier, were resumed[6]. These initiatives might have alleviated the tensions in the USD and EUR LIBOR-OIS spreads associated with the onset of the debt crisis, which caused no significant causality between the spreads at both the mean and variance levels.

Our empirical results can provide valuable insights to monetary authorities. Notably, we find that the directions and lags of the mean and the volatility spillover effects were different during the global financial crisis. This illustrates the importance of investigating the causality among the USD and EUR LIBOR-OIS spreads at the variance level as well as at the mean level. As the causality-in-variance can capture information flows, monitoring it thoroughly will help policymakers to understand the root causes of the apparent instability spreading across interbank markets, reflected in the simultaneous increases in LIBOR-OIS spreads of several currencies.

5.4. Conclusion

We investigate, for the first time, causality-in-variance, as well as causality-in-mean between the USD and EUR LIBOR-OIS spreads, employing the CCF approach advocated by Hong (2001). The approach allows for flexible specifications of innovation processes and is suitable for analysing the short-term, lead-lag relationships of volatility and mean transmissions between variables in a bivariate framework. We obtain the following results from our analysis: 1) a significant bi-directional causality-in-mean emerges during the global financial crisis period, consistent with the results of previous literature. 2) We find significant unidirectional causality-in-variance from the EUR to the USD spreads during the global financial crisis, indicating information flows presumably driven by the funding behaviours of European financial institutions. 3) Interestingly, we detect no significant causality-in-mean or causality-in-variance between the spreads during the European sovereign debt crisis period, supporting the view that the measures of the central banks were effective in alleviating liquidity tensions and avoiding transmissions between the LIBOR-OIS spreads. Our results provide useful insights, especially for the monetary authorities who aim to maintain liquidity in the money markets.

Notes

1 LIBOR is an indicative rate set in 10 currencies and for several maturities. It is published by the British Bankers' Association and widely used as a benchmark for interbank interest rates.
2 OIS is the rate underlying the interest rate swap contracts, where two parties agree to exchange the difference between accrued interests at a fixed rate with interests accrued through the geometric average of the floating index rate at maturity.
3 See Nelson (1991) for the EGARCH model.
4 See Hong (2001) for a detailed explanation on the methodology. The approach is typically used in a bi-variate framework, because it allows for analyzing only two variables at a time.
5 For instance, the causality-in-mean from the USD to EUR up to 15 lags is significant at the 1% level, while the direction from EUR to the USD is significant only at the 5% level.
6 Cour-Thimann and Winkler (2013) explain the details of such non-standard monetary policies implemented in responses to the surge of market expectations about a possible default of Greece. Our sample ends in June 2011 and thus, excludes the more drastic measures enacted after mid-2011; for instance, the 3-year long-term refinancing operations (LTROs).

References

Cheung, Y., Ng, L. (1996) A causality-in-variance test and its applications to financial market prices, *Journal of Econometrics*, **72**, 33–48.
Cour-Thimann, P., Winkler, B. (2013) The ECB's non-standard monetary policy measures. The role of institutional factors and financial structure, ECB Working Paper no. 1528, European Central Bank, Frankfurt.
Engle, R., Ito, T., Lin, W.L. (1990) Meteor showers or heat waves? Heteroskedastic intra-daily volatility in the foreign exchange market, *Econometrica*, **58**, 525–542.
Hong, Y. (2001) A test for volatility spillover with application to exchange rates, *Journal of Econometrics*, **103**, 183–224.
Imakubo, K., Kimura, T., Nagano, T. (2008) Cross-currency transmission of money market tensions, Bank of Japan Review E–2, Bank of Japan, Tokyo.
Ji, P.I., In, F. (2010) The impact of the global financial crisis on the cross-currency linkage of LIBOR-OIS spreads, *Journal of International Financial Market, Institutions, and Money*, **20**, 575–589.
Kwan, S. (2009) Behavior of Libor in the current financial crisis, *FRBSF Economic Letter*, Federal Reserve Bank of San Francisco, San Francisco, CA.
Kyle, A. (1985) Continuous auctions and insider trading, *Econometrica*, **53**, 1315–1335.
Kyle, A., Xiong, W. (2001) Contagion as a wealth effect, *Journal of Finance*, **56**, 1401–1440.

Michaud, F., Upper, C. (2008) What drives interbank rates? Evidence from the Libor panel, *BIS Quarterly Review*, **3**, 47–58.

Nelson, D. (1991) Conditional heteroskedasticity in asset returns: a new approach, *Econometrica*, **59**, 347–370.

Ross, S.A. (1989) Information and volatility: no-arbitrage Martingale approach to timing and resolution irrelevancy, *Journal of Finance*, **44**, 1–17.

Taylor, J.B., Williams, J.C. (2008) Further results on a black swan in the money market, Stanford Institute for Economic Policy Research Discussion Paper 7–46, Stanford Institute for Economic Policy Research, Stanford, CA.

6 Causality between the Euro and Greek sovereign CDS spreads

6.1. Introduction

In this chapter, we investigate the lead-lag relationships between the value of the euro and the Greek sovereign credit default swap (CDS) spreads, with a focus on uncovering the impact of the recent European sovereign debt crisis. A sovereign CDS is a swap contract in which a credit protection seller pays compensation to a protection buyer if a sovereign borrower experiences a pre-defined credit event. It has been used extensively as a market indicator, measuring the credit risk of the underlying issuer. After the outbreak of the debt crisis in late 2009, when credit rating agencies announced a series of downgrades for Greece, its sovereign CDS spreads increased sharply and the upward movement persisted through 2010 to 2011. Interestingly, the deterioration of Greece's creditworthiness, as reflected in the increases of its sovereign CDS spreads, was accompanied by the devaluation of the euro, which also began in November 2009. The downward pressure on the euro eased to some extent after the first bailout package for Greece was agreed to by the euro-area member states and the IMF in May 2010. Yet, its effect did not last, as the value of the currency dropped again in late 2010.

With the coincidence of the soaring Greek sovereign CDS spreads and the depreciation of the euro, it is interesting to see what theoretical rationale can explain a potential linkage between a sovereign CDS and the value of a currency. On one hand, a devaluation of a currency may have a negative effect on the credit risk of a country due to the occurrence of capital flight triggered by the devaluation (Ferrucci, 2003). Moreover, Bordo et al. (2009) contend that a sudden fall of the exchange rate might result in a reduced capacity of a country to repay debt denominated in a foreign currency and thus increase the country's default risk when its revenues are mostly in the local currency (i.e. in the presence of a currency mismatch). Hence, the value of the currency may affect sovereign CDS spreads.

On the other hand, causality in the reverse direction can be also considered. Zhang et al. (2010) argue that an increase in a country's credit risk might have an influence on the value of a currency because investors would call on a higher risk premium for that currency. This explanation is in line with the financial theory that the price of a financial asset should depend on its risk. Additionally, Maltritz (2008) shows, based on an option-pricing approach, that high indebtedness of countries could raise the probability of a currency crisis and hence may result in a currency devaluation. Thus, we expect that increases in the sovereign CDS spreads can have an adverse effect on the movement of the exchange rate, especially in times of sovereign debt crises.

Despite the existence of potential causality in both directions, at least theoretically as outlined above, there is limited empirical evidence on how sovereign CDS and exchange rates are interconnected. Hence, it is worth investigating the relationship empirically in the context of the recent debt crisis, when we observed soaring sovereign CDS spreads in Greece, the country where the crisis originated.

Recently there has been a growing body of literature about sovereign CDSs as they garner greater attention from academics as well as practitioners. Most previous studies have primarily analysed interrelationships between sovereign CDSs and bond markets (e.g. Fontana and Scheicher, 2010; Delis and Mylonidis, 2011; Palladini and Portes, 2011), between sovereign CDSs and banking CDS markets (Ejsing and Lemke, 2009; Acharya et al., 2011; Alter and Schüler, 2012), and between sovereign CDSs of different countries (e.g. Kalbaska and Gatkowski, 2012; Wang and Moore, 2012; Fong and Wong, 2012). Yet, only a limited number of studies touch upon linkages between a sovereign CDS and the value of a currency. To our knowledge, we think that the following two empirical works are comparable to our analysis in particular.

Liu and Morley (2012) study the relationship between 2- and 9-year sovereign CDS spreads for the US (from March 2008 to September 2010) and France (from August 2005 to September 2010), nominal effective exchange rates, and risk-free interest rates represented by the 3-month LIBOR. Employing the Granger causality tests in a standard VAR framework, they find that the exchange rates significantly led the sovereign CDS spreads for both the US and France, although the impact of the interest rates on the sovereign CDS was limited. They also detect significant causality from the sovereign CDS to the exchange rate in the case for France.

Using data for the period from July 2006 to September 2010, Eichler (2012) assesses the potential impact of the sovereign debt crisis risk (as measured by the 10-year sovereign CDS spreads and bond yield spreads) on the euro/US dollar exchange rate. With a generalized autoregressive conditional heteroskedasticity (GARCH) model, he finds evidence of the euro's depreciation against the US dollar when the debt crisis risk increases. Further, his analysis reveals that the value of the euro is more negatively influenced by the sovereign debt crisis risk in GIIPS countries (Greece, Ireland, Italy, Portugal, and Spain) than in relatively stable countries (Austria, Belgium, France, Germany, and the Netherlands).

This study is along the lines of Liu and Morley (2012), but primarily contributes to the existing literature by focusing on analysing how the long- and the short-run relationships between the sovereign CDS spreads for Greece and the euro were altered in the wake of the recent debt crisis. Ours differs from Eichler (2012), who assumes only a one-way causality, from the sovereign CDS spreads to the exchange rate movement, in terms of allowing for a two-way causality between the variables. Our use of Toda and Yamamoto's (1995) lag-augmented VAR (LA-VAR) method enables us to avoid potential bias from diagnostic testing of cointegration and demonstrates the significant long-run causality from the euro to the Greek sovereign CDS only after the onset of the debt crisis. The generalized impulse response function (G-IRF) analysis, which is robust to variable orderings in the VAR system, reveals some evidence of the short-run effect running in that direction as well.

The rest of this chapter is organized as follows. Section 6.2 reviews our empirical methods. Section 6.3 explains our dataset. Section 6.4 reports the estimation results, and Section 6.5 concludes the chapter.

6.2. Empirical methodology

A conventional VAR model or the vector error correction model (VECM) is often used when there is a need to investigate causal relationships between the series. When using these models, we need to execute pre-testing for assessing the existence of cointegration. Nonetheless, it is widely known that various kinds of diagnostic tests tend to produce different results. Hence, a bias that arises in these tests may lead to problems in statistical inference in the subsequent causality analysis based on the VAR or VECM framework. In order to overcome such problems, Toda and Yamaomoto (1995) propose the LA-VAR approach, which enables us to perform long-run Granger causality tests between the series in a level VAR system without necessitating pre-testing for cointegration. Further, the approach can be used regardless of the order of integration of the series. In light of these benefits, we use the LA-VAR methodology in this study.

In Toda and Yamamoto's LA-VAR procedure, the maximum integration order (d) of the series is first determined and then added to the optimum lag length (k) in order to 'augment' the VAR (k) system in levels. We can perform a modified Wald test on the first k parameters of a LA-VAR $(k + d)$ system for an n-vector time series $\{y_t\}$, which is described as

$$y_t = a_0 + A_1 y_{t-1} + \ldots + A_p y_{t-p} + \varepsilon_t,$$

(1)

where p is equal to the true lag length (k) plus the maximum integration order (d) and ε_t is a white noise residual. Note that d must not exceed the optimal lag length k. According to Toda and Yamamoto (1995), the Wald test statistic on the first k parameters in (1) has an asymptotic chi-square distribution with k degrees of freedom. If the Wald test statistic is found to be significant, we will conclude that the null hypothesis of no Granger causality between the series is rejected.

The Granger causality test in the above LA-VAR framework is useful for examining a relatively long-run static relationship between the series. In order to see short-run responses of each variable to shocks in other variables and the persistence of the effects, we also employ a G-IRF analysis[1]. In contrast to a standard orthogonalized approach, in which results usually vary when we change the order of variables in the system, the G-IRF approach is not sensitive to variable ordering. Note that both methodologies produce the same results when the covariance matrix is diagonal.

6.3. Data

Daily data from 2 January 2008 to 30 December 2011 is used, with 1,027 observations in total. We use the 5-year sovereign CDS spread data for Greece (CDS hereafter), which is the most actively traded amongst the various maturities. The sovereign CDS spreads are expressed in basis points. Similar to Liu and Morley (2012), we employ the nominal effective exchange rate (NEER) for the euro (EUR). This index is based on weighted averages of bilateral euro exchange rates against 20 trading partners of the Eurozone. The increase in the value of NEER implies that more foreign currency can be obtained for 1 euro on average. As a control variable in our LA-VAR system, we also include the 3-month euro LIBOR (INT), which can be regarded as the risk-free interest rate in the Eurozone. All data are extracted from Thomson Reuters Datastream. The beginning date is constrained by the availability of the Greek sovereign CDS spreads[2].

We divide the whole sample into two sub-sample periods: Sample A (the period from 2 January 2008 to 4 November 2009) and Sample B (the period from 5 November 2009 to 30 December 2011). Sample B denotes the debt crisis period, given the fact that in early November 2009, the Greece government's disclosure of the real size of its fiscal deficit, far larger than what had been previously announced, raised doubts of market participants about the solvency of the nation. Sample A is viewed as the pre-crisis period, before the Greek debt crisis began.

Figure 6.1 plots movements of CDS and EUR in logarithm form over the entire sample. We see that since November 2009, the Greek sovereign CDS spreads persistently followed an upward trend, whilst the value of the euro (as

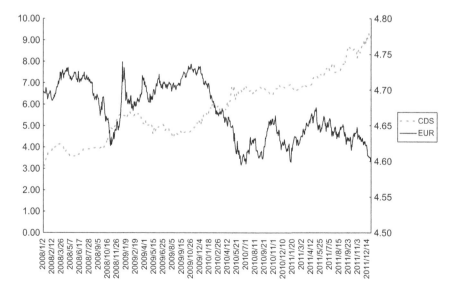

Figure 6.1 Movement of the Greek CDS spreads and the NEER for the euro

represented by NEER) contrastively exhibited a depreciation pressure by moving upward and downward after May 2010 (but did not return to the levels of the pre-crisis period).

Table 6.1 reports descriptive statistics of our data in logarithm form. It is worthwhile to mention that there are sharp increases in the standard deviation between Samples A and B for both CDS and EUR. This indicates that the increased market uncertainty created by the debt crisis increased volatilities of

Table 6.1 Summary of statistics

	CDS	EUR	INT
Entire sample			
Mean	5.8167	4.6696	−0.8684
Median	5.6095	4.6668	−0.9349
Maximum	9.3141	4.7392	0.6695
Minimum	3.0865	4.5949	−2.3846
SD	1.4656	0.0383	0.6547
Skewness	0.2670	−0.0398	0.2972
Kurtosis	2.2308	1.6999	2.0906
Jarque–Bera	37.5***	72.6***	50.5***
Sample A (Pre-crisis period)			
Mean	4.5186	4.6984	−0.4195
Median	4.6347	4.7044	−0.4423
Maximum	5.6664	4.7392	0.6695
Minimum	3.0865	4.6218	−1.5517
SD	0.6590	0.0236	0.5017
Skewness	0.0010	−1.0892	0.0918
Kurtosis	1.7803	3.9762	2.7150
Jarque–Bera	29.3***	112.1***	2.3
Sample B (Crisis period)			
Mean	6.9206	4.6452	−1.2502
Median	6.7716	4.6401	−1.4060
Maximum	9.3141	4.7327	−0.0706
Minimum	4.8870	4.5949	−2.3846
SD	0.9758	0.0306	0.5121
Skewness	0.3825	1.0585	1.0095
Kurtosis	2.8595	3.9086	3.0615
Jarque–Bera	14.0***	122.7***	94.4***

Notes: Statistics for log-transformed data are reported.

*** denotes statistical significance at the 1% level.

Table 6.2 Results of ADF unit root tests

Variable	Specification	Sample A: Pre-crisis period		Sample B: Crisis period	
		Test statistic	p-value	Test statistic	p-value
Levels					
CDS	Intercept	−2.0473	0.2666	−0.3403	0.9161
	Intercept and trend	−1.4343	0.8498	−2.1039	0.5420
EUR	Intercept	−1.8747	0.3443	−2.3970	0.1430
	Intercept and trend	−1.9171	0.6439	−2.3023	0.4315
INT	Intercept	0.1952	0.9721	−1.0104	0.7510
	Intercept and trend	−0.3824	0.9880	−1.8326	0.6877
First-differences					
CDS	Intercept	−17.5087***	0.0000	−20.9968***	0.0000
	Intercept and trend	−17.6406***	0.0000	−20.9820***	0.0000
EUR	Intercept	−21.8445***	0.0000	−21.9936***	0.0000
	Intercept and trend	−21.8323***	0.0000	−21.9955***	0.0000
INT	Intercept	−14.5905***	0.0000	−30.1048***	0.0000
	Intercept and trend	−22.2140***	0.0000	−30.1174***	0.0000

*** denotes statistical significance at the 1% level.

the Greek sovereign CDS spreads and the euro substantially. Table 6.1 also shows that the Jarque–Bera test rejects normality for all variables, except for INT in Sample A.

The ADF test is employed to check for the order of integration of the series. The results of the ADF test are presented in Table 6.2, indicating that for both Samples A and B, the first-differenced data for CDS, EUR, and INT with intercept or with intercept and trend are stationary and thus they are all I(1) variables[3]. Thus, we determine that the maximum integration order (*d*) is one.

6.4.   Empirical results

We assess causal relationships between the Greek sovereign CDS spreads and the value of the euro, with the interest rate (the euro LIBOR) as a control variable, in the LA-VAR framework. First, the optimum lag length is chosen based on the Akaike Information Criterion and Schwarz Bayesian Information Criterion. The results show that the optimum lag length (*k*) is one for Sample A and two for Sample B. We conduct the Breusch–Godfrey Lagrange Multiplier test to check for serial correlation and confirm that there is no autocorrelation in the VAR residuals. Adding the maximum integration order of one (*d* = 1), we set the total lag length (*p*) as two for Sample A and three for Sample B.

Table 6.3 Results of Granger causality tests in LA-VAR framework

Investigated	Sample A: Pre-crisis period			Sample B: Crisis period		
Causality	k+d	Wald statistic	p-value	k+d	Wald statistic	p-value
CDS→EUR		1.2144	0.2705		0.7675	0.6813
EUR→CDS		1.4537	0.2279		7.3610**	0.0252
CDS→INT		0.3920	0.5312		1.1051	0.5755
INT→CDS	2	0.3299	0.5657	3	0.4147	0.8127
EUR→INT		0.1000	0.7518		1.4779	0.4776
INT→EUR		3.1630*	0.0753		19.5970***	0.0001

***, **, and * denote statistical significance at the 1%, 5%, and 10% levels, respectively.

Now, we investigate the long-run Granger causality between the series. Table 6.3 displays results for the Granger causality tests in Samples A and B, which reveals several interesting findings. In Sample A (the pre-crisis period), no significant Granger causality was identified between the Greek sovereign CDS spreads and the euro. Contrastively, in Sample B (the debt crisis period), the euro significantly Granger causes the Greek sovereign CDS spreads at the 5% level, although no significant causality in the opposite direction was found. On the other hand, we did not find significant causality between the euro LIBOR and the sovereign CDS spreads in both Samples A and B. These results imply that the exchange rate movement was a more important driving factor for the Greek sovereign CDS than that for the risk-free interest rate, especially in the time of the debt crisis. This is in line with the results of Liu and Morley (2012), who find evidence of the exchange rates having an influence on the 2- and 9-year sovereign CDS spreads for France and the US using a sample period which includes the recent financial crises. In terms of the possibility of the reverse causality, our results also demonstrate that we could not extract information to predict the nominal effective exchange rate for the euro from the movement of the Greek sovereign CDS spreads.

Our next step is to conduct the G-IRF analysis to investigate whether there are any short-run effects between the variables. Figure 6.2 and 6.3 show the generalized impulse responses of each variable to a one-standard deviation shock to other variables together with two standard error bands. Figure 6.2 indicates that during the pre-crisis period, the response of the CDS spreads to the shocks in both the euro and the euro LIBOR were not significant. However, as exhibited in Figure 6.3, we find that during the crisis period, the initial response of the CDS spreads to the euro was significantly negative (i.e. the lower the NEER was for the euro, the higher the Greek sovereign CDS spreads became), although the effect was not persistent and gradually died out after the third month. In contrast, neither the response of the CDS spreads to shocks in the interest rate nor those of the euro and the interest rate to shocks in the CDS spreads were

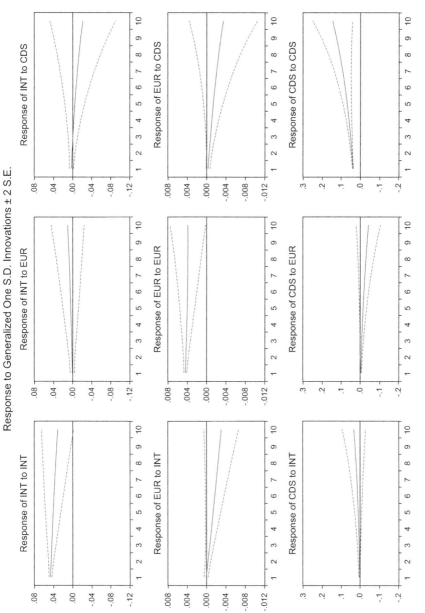

Figure 6.2 Generalized impulse responses to a one-standard deviation shock (pre-crisis period)

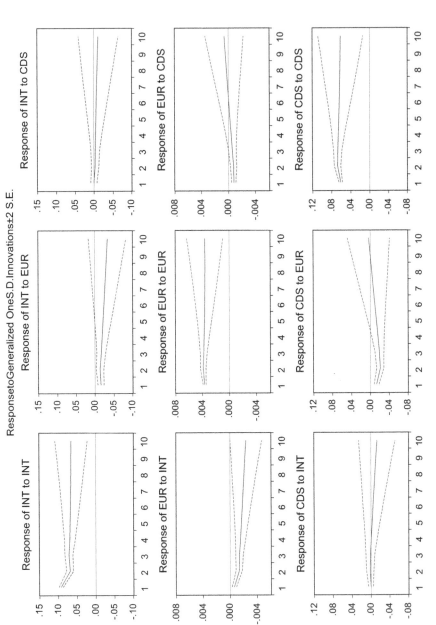

Figure 6.3 Generalized impulse responses to a one-standard deviation shock (crisis period)

significant. These results are consistent with those of our long-run Granger causality tests and thus provide support for the role of the euro in affecting the Greek sovereign CDS spreads in times of crisis.

Overall, our findings based on the long- and short-run analysis suggest that the value of the euro during the debt crisis period was significantly transmitted to the Greek sovereign CDS spreads. One possible reason is that perhaps investors perceived that the declining value of the euro lowered chances for Greece to repay its public debts, which may have resulted in the increased credit risk of the country. As the euro depreciated and investors' confidence in the single currency waned, capital flight from Greece occurred, affecting the country's creditworthiness as well. On the other hand, our analysis reveals that there was no significant causality running from the Greek sovereign CDS spreads to the euro. This is in contrast to the results of Eichler (2012), who used a GARCH model and detected evidence of the aggregated measure of the sovereign CDS spreads for GIIPS countries affecting the euro exchange rate against the US dollar during the debt crisis. The non-causality from the sovereign CDS spreads to the euro in our analysis may have been partially due to the lower size and liquidity of the Greek sovereign CDS markets alone.

Based on our empirical results, we can draw important implications for policymakers and investors. Firstly, monitoring variability in the exchange rate is crucial for countries such as Greece that have concerns over increased credit risks triggered by market turbulence. Policy measures to stabilize the risks should address minimizing the potential adverse effects of the transmission of the exchange rate movements to the sovereign CDS markets. Secondly, the sovereign CDS spreads for Greece, the country where the European debt crisis originated, are not necessarily useful indicators for investors trying to predict the euro exchange rate for hedging and speculative purposes. Our long-run causality analysis indicates that the 3-month euro LIBOR may have more valuable information than the sovereign CDS spreads for the prediction of currency movements.

6.5. Conclusion

This study examined the causal relationships among the 5-year Greek sovereign CDS spreads, the nominal effective exchange rate for the euro, and the 3-month euro LIBOR for the period from 2 January 2008 to 30 December 2011. Our use of the LA-VAR method enabled us to test for the long-run Granger-causality between the series without conducting prior tests of cointegration and thus avoided diagnostic testing bias. Further, we also employed the G-IRF analysis, which is robust to the ordering of the variables in the VAR system, in order to identify short-run effects in responses to shocks in other variables.

Our key findings are summarized as follows. First, during the debt crisis period, the value of the euro significantly affected the Greek sovereign CDS spreads, suggesting that the devaluation of the euro increased the perceived credit risks of the Greek economy. Our G-IRF analysis identified the short-run temporary effect and thus reinforced such a significant unidirectional causality. Second, during both the pre-crisis and crisis periods, there was no significant causality running from the Greek sovereign CDS spreads to the euro, implying that the sovereign CDS spreads did not contain useful information to help predict the currency market. Third, the euro LIBOR, as a proxy for the risk-free interest rate, significantly Granger-caused the value of the euro. These results may be helpful for policymakers and investors who want to gain insights on the interrelationships between the growing sovereign CDS markets and macroeconomic variables such as the exchange rate and the short-term interest rate.

Notes

1 See Koop et al. (1996) and Pesaran and Shin (1998) for the detailed explanation of the generalized impulse response function methodology.
2 Datastream provides the 5-year sovereign CDS spread data for Greece only from 16 December 2007 onwards.
3 We also applied the Phillips and Perron test and the Kwiatkowski, Phillips, Schmidt, and Shin test for a robustness check and confirmed that the conclusions were similar. The results are not reported here for the sake of brevity.

References

Acharya, V., Drechsler, I., Schnabl, P. (2011) A Pyrrhic victory? Bank bailouts and sovereign credit risk, NBER Working Paper no. 17136, National Bureau of Economic Research, Cambridge, MA.

Alter, A., Schüler, Y. S. (2012) Credit spread interdependencies of European states and banks during the financial crisis, *Journal of Banking and Finance*, **36**, 3444–3468.

Bordo, M., Meissner, C., Weidenmier, M. (2009) Identifying the effects of an exchange rate depreciation on country risk: Evidence from a natural experiment, *Journal of International Money and Finance*, **28**, 1022–1044.

Delis, M. D., Mylonidis, N. (2011) The chicken or the egg? A note on the dynamic interrelation between government bond spreads and credit default swaps, *Finance Research Letters*, **8**, 163–170.

Eichler, S. (2012) The impact of banking and sovereign debt crisis risk in the eurozone on the euro/US dollar exchange rate, *Applied Financial Economics*, **22**, 1215–1232.

Ejsing, J.W., Lemke, W. (2009) The Janus-headed salvation: sovereign and bank credit risk premia during 2008–2009, ECB Working Paper no. 1127, European Central Bank, Frankfurt.

Ferrucci, G. (2003) Empirical determinants of emerging market economies' sovereign bond spreads, Bank of England Working Paper no. 205, Bank of England, London.

Fong, T., Wong, A. (2012) Gauging potential sovereign risk contagion in Europe, *Economics Letters*, **115**, 496–499.

Fontana, A., Scheicher, M. (2010) An analysis of Euro area sovereign CDS and their relation with government bonds, ECB Working Paper no. 1271, European Central Bank, Frankfurt.

Kalbaska, A., Gatkowski, M. (2012) Eurozone sovereign contagion: Evidence from the CDS market (2005–2010), *Journal of Economic Behavior and Organization*, **83**, 657–673.

Koop, G., Pesaran, M.H., Potter, S.M. (1996) Impulse response analysis in nonlinear multivariate models, *Journal of Econometrics*, **74**, 119–147.

Liu, Y., Morley, B. (2012) Sovereign credit default swaps and the macroeconomy, *Applied Economics Letters*, **19**, 129–132.

Maltritz, D. (2008) Modelling the dependency between currency and debt crises: an option based approach, *Economics Letters*, **100**, 344–347.

Pesaran, M.H., Shin, Y. (1998) Generalized impulse response analysis in linear multivariate models, *Economic Letters*, **58**, 17–29.

Palladini, G., Portes, R. (2011) Sovereign CDS and bond pricing dynamics in the euro-area, NBER Working Paper no. 17586, National Bureau of Economic Research, Cambridge, MA.

Toda, H.Y., Yamamoto, T. (1995) Statistical inference in vector autoregressions with possibly near integrated processes, *Journal of Econometrics*, **66**, 225–250.

Wang, P., Moore, T. (2012) The integration of the credit default swap markets during the US subprime crisis: Dynamic correlation analysis, *Journal of International Financial Markets, Institutions, and Money*, **22**, 1–15.

Zhang, G., Yau, J., Fung, H.G. (2010) Do credit default swaps predict currency values? *Applied Financial Economics*, **20**, 439–458.

Part III

When did structural changes in financial markets occur due to the crisis?

7 Structural breaks in the volatility of the Greek sovereign bond index

7.1. Introduction

The large shocks to the Greek sovereign bond markets during the recent European debt crisis stunned the market participants. This is primarily because there is a convention of treating government bonds as risk-free instruments, based on a sovereign entity's ability to either raise taxes, cut spending, print money, or some combination of the three. Until recently, government debt instruments in developed nations had been regarded as a proxy for the unobservable risk-free rate (e.g. Blanco et al., 2005; Delis and Mylonidis, 2011). Since the introduction of the Euro and until the onset of the recent financial crises, many investors believed Eurozone government bonds behaved as if they were free of country-specific risks (e.g. Oliveira et al., 2012).

The present study examines the implications of excess volatility in the sovereign bond markets on the decision-making of both investors and policymakers. First, extreme volatility may disrupt the investors' abilities to forecast and manage the interest risk of assets held in their portfolio. This is a significant issue, especially for those traders constructing a portfolio whose value could be directly affected by interest rate variability. Second, a striking increase in volatility disrupts the smooth functioning of the financial system because financial institutions holding substantial amounts of sovereign bonds may suffer from potential impairment losses. Indeed, this was observed for major European banks during the period of the debt crisis. A sudden change in bond yield volatility may motivate policymakers to consider the introduction of new regulatory schemes. Given the importance of excess volatility, we explore empirical models of time-varying conditional volatility for the 10-year Greek government bond returns within a regime-switching framework.

Many studies have modelled volatility by controlling for structural changes in the case of stock returns (e.g. Cunado et al., 2004; Malik et al., 2005; Hammoudeh and Li, 2008; Wang and Moore, 2009), exchange rate returns (e.g. Malik, 2003; Rapach and Strauss, 2008), and the real gross domestic product (GDP) growth (e.g. Cecchetti et al., 2006; Fang and Miller, 2008, 2009). However, few studies have focused on investigating the suddenness of volatility changes in sovereign bond markets.

A rare example is Covarrubias et al. (2006), who modelled the volatility of the 10-year US Treasury note and detected its structural changes using the iterated cumulative sums of squares algorithm. They found that the identified regime shifts were associated with major economic events and that the volatility persistence measure in a GARCH model[1] largely decreased when considering such regime shifts. Moreover, their empirical results indicated that a volatility model based on GARCH, controlling for structural breaks, was superior when performing out-of-sample forecasts.

To our knowledge, this study is the first to examine structural changes in the volatility of sovereign bond index returns in the context of the European debt crisis. We focus on the 10-year sovereign bond yields of Greece, the origin of the debt crisis, covering the sample period from April 1999 to March 2012. We use the multiple structural change test of Bai and Perron (1998, 2003) to detect the break dates in volatility and incorporate them into an exponential GARCH (EGARCH) model[2]. One of the major advantages of this methodology is that it allows for estimating multiple structural changes endogenously. It also enables us to generalize specifications, for example, to select whether to allow for heterogeneity and autocorrelation in the residuals.

Our results show that for the Greek government bond returns, the structural break date in the variance and mean is April 2010. Incorporating structural break dummy variables into our EGARCH-based model results in superior estimation results, and the positively significant coefficient of the dummy variable of a structural break in variance suggests that the regime shift was triggered by the European sovereign debt crisis. Moreover, we find that the measure of volatility persistence decreases substantially when incorporating the structural change into our model, which is consistent with the finding of Covarrubias et al. (2006)[3].

The rest of this chapter is organized as follows. Section 7.2 provides a brief explanation of our dataset. Section 7.3 describes our empirical findings. Section 7.4 concludes.

7.2.   Data

Our dataset contains monthly returns of the Greek 10-year benchmark bond index (B_t), between April 1999 and March 2012 and includes 156 observations[4]. All data are sourced from Datastream. The ADF test was used to test the null hypothesis of a unit root, yielding evidence that the series were I (1) variables[5]. Hence, hereafter we focus on the monthly changes in bond indices; the bond index returns (b_t) are calculated as the difference of the logarithm of the bond indices multiplied by 100.

Table 7.1 displays a summary of the descriptive statistics for the monthly Greek bond index returns. The standard deviation, or the volatility of bond index returns, is 5.10. The negative value of skewness (-2.59) indicates that decreases are more likely to occur than increases. A high kurtosis (13.09) means that substantial changes occur more frequently, suggesting the existence of fat tails in the return distribution. Moreover, the Jarque–Bera test rejects normality for the series at the 5% significance level.

Table 7.1 Basic statistics for returns of the 10-year Greek government bond index

	Mean(%)	Max(%)	Min(%)	SD	Skewness	Kurtosis	Jarque–Bera
b_t	−0.95	11.67	−29.81	5.10	−2.59	13.09	830.96**

Notes: Statistics for the logarithmic difference of the monthly data multiplied by 100 (to express a percentage) are reported.

** denotes statistical significance at the 5% level.

7.3. Empirical results

AR-EGARCH (or AR-GARCH) specification

We first employ the autoregressive (AR) model for the bond return series. Using the Bayesian Information Criterion (BIC), we select the AR(1) process for the conditional mean equation, denoted by

$$b_t = a_0 + a_1 b_{t-1} + \varepsilon_t. \tag{1}$$

As for the conditional variance of returns, we use the EGARCH model for the following reasons. First, the coefficients of the ARCH terms in the EGARCH model can capture the asymmetric effects of positive and negative shocks. This may provide a good fit to the test in this chapter, because previous studies have reported that the volatility in bond returns tends to exhibit asymmetric movement, implying that the shocks to volatility differ depending on whether the bond index returns increase or decrease[6]. Second, the logarithmic form of the EGARCH model ensures the non-negativity of the conditional variance. Hence, the EGARCH model is preferable to other forms of asymmetric, conditional volatility models, such as the Glosten-Jagannathan-Runkle GARCH (GJR-GARCH) model proposed by Glosten et al. (1993), in which we are constrained by the signs of the coefficients. The EGARCH(1,1) model is described as follows:

$$\log(\sigma_t^2) = \omega + (\alpha_1 |z_{t-1}| + \gamma_1 z_{t-1}) + \beta_1 \log(\sigma_{t-1}^2), \tag{2}$$

where $z_t = \varepsilon_t/\sigma_t$. As the sample data exhibits excess kurtosis, we estimate the model using the maximum likelihood estimation technique, assuming t-distributed errors. The sign of the coefficient γ_1 captures the asymmetric effect of positive and negative innovations. Coefficient β_1 represents the marginal contribution of the lagged conditional variance to conditional variance at time t and can be regarded as a measure of 'first-order' volatility persistence[7].

For comparison, we also employ the GARCH(1,1) specification, the most commonly used model of financial asset return volatility, for the conditional variance equation, where

$$\sigma_t^2 = \omega + \alpha_1 \varepsilon_{t-1}^2 + \beta_1 \sigma_{t-1}^2. \tag{3}$$

Unlike the EGARCH framework, the GARCH model is constrained by the coefficients' signs (i.e. $\alpha_1 \geq 0$, $\beta_1 \geq 0$, and $\alpha_1 + \beta_1 < 1$), to ensure stability of the conditional variances; $\alpha_1 + \beta_1$, the sum of the estimated ARCH and GARCH parameters, represents a measure of volatility persistence, as contended by Fang and Miller (2008) and Fang and Miller (2009)[8].

Table 7.2 shows the estimation results of the two specifications. The AR(1)–EGARCH(1, 1) model yields the better specification for several reasons. Its variance equation shows a reasonably good fit to the data, with all parameters, except the coefficient γ_1, significant at the 10% level[9]. The maximum log-likelihood value is also higher. Moreover, the *p*-values of the Ljung–Box statistics imply no autocorrelation up to order 12 for standardized residuals and standard residuals squared. It is worthwhile to emphasize that this EGARCH specification resulted in a very high value of our 'first-order' volatility persistence measure ($\beta_1 = 1.0167$), whose validity we examine in the following analysis.

Incorporating structural changes

Similar to Fang and Miller (2009), we employ a two-step procedure to identify structural break points in the mean and volatility of Greek bond index returns. First, we apply the Bai and Perron (1998, 2003) approach[10] to the AR(1) model in Equation (1) to find multiple structural breaks for the mean of b_t. We specifically use a sequential application of the Sup F $(k + 1|k)$ statistics to find $k + 1$ breaks, conditional upon identifying k breaks. We obtain the residuals $\hat{\varepsilon}_t$ from

Table 7.2 Model estimation: AR-EGARCH versus AR-GARCH

	AR(1)-EGARCH(1,1) specification		
	Conditional mean equation: $b_t = a_0 + a_1 b_{t-1} + \varepsilon_t$		
	Conditional variance equation: $\log(\sigma_t^2) = \omega + (\alpha_1 \lvert z_{t-1} \rvert + \gamma_1 z_{t-1}) + \beta_1 \log(\sigma_{t-1}^2)$		
	Estimate	*SE*	p-*value*
a_0	0.0214	0.1404	0.8786
a_1	0.0905	0.0820	0.2693
ω	−0.1769**	0.0676	0.0089
α_1	0.2297**	0.0938	0.0143
γ_1	−0.0661	0.0761	0.3853
β_1	1.0167**	0.0189	0.0000
Log-likelihood	−347.9430		
$Q(12)$	6.8797		
p-value	0.8650		
$Q^2(12)$	6.8711		
p-value	0.8660		

	AR(1)-GARCH(1,1) specification Conditional mean equation: $b_t = a_0 + a_1 b_{t-1} + \varepsilon_t$ Conditional variance equation: $\sigma_t^2 = \omega + \alpha_1 \varepsilon_{t-1}^2 + \beta_1 \sigma_{t-1}^2$		
	Estimate	*SE*	*p-value*
a_0	0.0886	0.1362	0.5153
a_1	0.0937	0.0893	0.2939
ω	0.0238	0.1427	0.8676
α_1	0.2180**	0.0997	0.0287
β_1	0.8446**	0.0912	0.0000
Log-likelihood	−349.0874		
$Q(12)$	5.8892		
p-value	0.9220		
$Q^2(12)$	6.2441		
p-value	0.9030		

Notes: $Q(12)$ and $Q^2(12)$ are the Ljung–Box Q statistics up to the 12th order.

** denote statistical significance at the 5% level.

this estimation process. Next, following Cecchetti et al. (2006), we identify breaks in the variance through Equation (4).

$$\sqrt{\pi/2}\left|\hat{\varepsilon}_t\right| = c + u_t, \tag{4}$$

where the transformed residuals on the left-hand side represent the unbiased estimators of the standard deviation of ε_t.

Table 7.3 reports the results of the structural break tests in the mean (Panel A) and variance (Panel B). Consider the existence of breaks displayed in Panel B, the focus of our analysis. The *Sup* F_T (k|0) statistics indicate significance at the 5% level for all k between 1 and 5, implying the presence of at least one structural break. The sequential *Sup* F_T (2|1) statistic is not significant, showing that only one structural break is detected in the variance of the bond index return series through the sequential process. From the Modified Schwarz Information Criterion (LWZ) and BIC, we also obtain one structural break. The identified break date is April 2010. Moreover, as shown in Panel A, we find that only one structural break exists in the mean, which is also April 2010.

The detection of this break date is interesting, because there is apparently no consensus in academic studies on when the European sovereign debt crisis commenced. For instance, Kasimati (2011) regarded 17 November 2009, when the Bank of Greece cautioned about the possibility of funding reduction from the European Central Bank, as the start of the crisis. In contrast, Tamakoshi (2011) chose 16 December 2009, when Standard & Poor's cut Greece's credit rating

Table 7.3 Empirical results of the Bai and Perron (1998, 2003) tests

Panel A. Structural break test in mean

Tests[1]

SupFT(1):	SupFT(2):	SupFT(3):	SupFT(4):	SupFT(5):
10.5044*	5.8156	3.7127	2.7370	2.0695
SupFT(2|1):	SupFT(3|2):	SupFT(4|3):	SupFT(5|4):	
2.8088	1.2174	0.2164	—	

Number of breaks selected

Sequential:	LWZ:	BIC:
1 break	1 break	1 break

Break date[2]

2010:4 (2006:11–2010:5)

Panel B. Structural break test in volatility

Tests[1]

SupFT(1):	SupFT(2):	SupFT(3):	SupFT(4):	SupFT(5):
37.4997**	22.8947**	16.7698**	14.0828**	11.1514**
SupFT(2|1):	SupFT(3|2):	SupFT(4|3):	SupFT(5|4):	
6.7759	4.0771	2.8646	1.0943	

Number of breaks selected

Sequential:	LWZ:	BIC:
1 break	1 break	1 break

Break date[2]

2010:4 (2009:9–2010:5)

Notes:

[1] We sequentially test for the hypothesis of k breaks vs. $k + 1$ breaks, employing the Sup FT($k + 1|k$) statistics.

[2] The 95% confidence intervals are shown in parentheses.

** denotes statistical significance at the 5% level.

from A1− to BBB+, declaring a negative outlook on national solvency. Our findings suggest that structural breaks in the mean and variance of the Greek bond return series occurred much later than these dates. In fact, in April 2010, the Greek sovereign debt was downgraded to junk bond status, resulting in heightened concerns across the Eurozone and the agreement of a €110 billion bailout loan for Greece on 2 May 2010. Figure 7.1 presents the performance of the Greek 10-year bond index, visually confirming that the fluctuations of the returns increased substantially after April 2010. Figure 7.2 also reports that the conditional variance of the bond index rose sharply after April 2010.

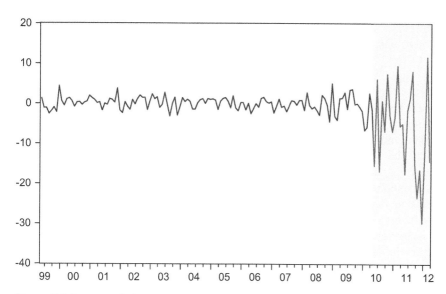

Figure 7.1 Returns of the 10-year Greek government bond index (percentage), April 1999–March 2012

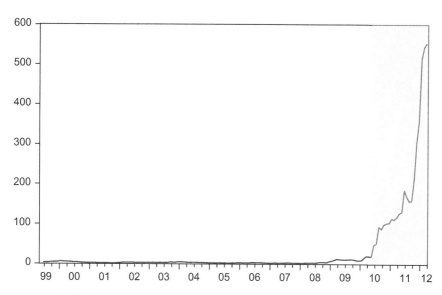

Figure 7.2 Conditional variances of the 10-year Greek government bond index, April 1999–March 2012

Now, since the structural break date is detected, we include in our AR (1)–EGARCH (1, 1) specification a dummy variable in the mean and variance equations as:

$$b_t = a_0 + a_1 b_{t-1} + d_1 D_1 + \varepsilon_t \text{ and} \tag{5}$$

$$\log(\sigma_t^2) = w + (\alpha_1 |z_{t-1}| + \gamma_1 z_{t-1}) + \beta_1 \log(\sigma_{t-1}^2) + d_2 D_2, \tag{6}$$

where both D_1 and D_2 equal 1 after the break date (April 2010) and 0 otherwise[11]. Table 7.4 indicates the estimation results of the AR (1)–EGARCH (1, 1) model with dummies in the mean and variance and provides three significant findings. First, the maximum log-likelihood value improved compared to the case in Table 7.2, suggesting that our inclusion of the two dummy variables yields better estimation results. Second, the coefficient of the dummy variable on the structural break in variance (d_2) is positively significant at the 5% level. This suggests that the high variance in the Greek bond return series after the break date represents a regime change triggered by the European debt crisis. Third, β_1, the coefficient representing the marginal contribution of the lagged conditional variance to

Table 7.4 Model estimation: AR–EGARCH with dummies in mean and variance

	AR(1)-EGARCH(1,1) with structural breaks		
	Conditional mean equation:		
	$b_t = a_0 + a_1 b_{t-1} + d_1 D_1 + \varepsilon_t$		
	Conditional variance equation:		
	$\log(\sigma_t^2) = w + (\alpha_1 |z_{t-1}| + \gamma_1 z_{t-1}) + \beta_1 \log(\sigma_{t-1}^2) + d_2 D_2$		
	Estimate	*SE*	*p-value*
a_0	0.0353	0.1513	0.8157
a_1	0.1027	0.0824	0.2127
d_1	−5.6246**	2.0390	0.0058
ω	0.2868	0.2690	0.2864
α_1	0.3299	0.2118	0.1193
γ_1	−0.3422**	0.1413	0.0155
β_1	0.4522	0.2828	0.1098
D_2	2.1020**	1.0962	0.0552
Log-likelihood	−340.4880		
Q(12)	7.7688		
p-value	0.8030		
Q²(12)	8.4504		
p-value	0.7490		

Notes: $Q(12)$ and $Q^2(12)$ are the Ljung–Box Q statistics up to the 12th order.

** denotes statistical significant at the 5% level.

conditional variance at t, is positive but no longer significant in the specification including the dummies, exhibiting a sharp decline in value from 1.0167 (Table 7.2) to 0.4522. Our finding that the measure of this 'first-order' volatility persistence is overestimated when using the EGARCH specification, without incorporating regime shifts in variance, is in line with Covarrubias et al. (2006).

7.4. Conclusion

In this chapter, we employ the Bai and Perron (1998, 2003) approach to test for multiple structural breaks in the mean and volatility of the 10-year Greek bond index return during the period from April 1999 to March 2012. We used the standard AR (1)–EGARCH (1, 1) specification to model the mean and variance equation. After the detection of the break date, we included dummy variables to incorporate a regime change. We derived four main findings: a) the detected break date in volatility is April 2010, when the Greek bond was downgraded to junk status; b) including structural break dummy variables yields superior estimation results; c) a positively significant coefficient of the dummy variable on structural break in variance implies a regime shift caused by the European debt crisis; and d) our measure of 'first-order' volatility persistence declines sharply after incorporating the structural break.

Our finding that a regime shift in the volatility of the Greek government bond indeed occurred provides implications to traders and policymakers for risk management. For traders, incorporating the structural change in modelling or forecasting the volatility of the sovereign bond is important to hedge the risk of their portfolios, which are exposed to the variability of interest rates. For policymakers, the knowledge on when and how the regime shift in the volatility took place is helpful for examining potential causes of the bond market's disruption and thereby forming appropriate regulatory measures to avoid future adverse effects.

Notes

1 See Bollerslev (1986) for details on the GARCH models.
2 See Nelson (1991) for details of the EGARCH models.
3 Covarrubias et al. (2006) find that the persistence of shocks, which is measured by the sum of the estimated ARCH and GARCH parameters, decreases substantially when the regime control variables were included in their GARCH model applied to the 10-year US Treasury note yields, from 4 April 1994 to 13 November 2001.
4 The beginning date is constrained by data availability, because Datastream provides the Greek 10-year bond index series only from April 1999 onwards.
5 The results of the unit root test are not reported here but are available upon request.
6 See, for example, De Goeij and Marquering (2004) and Cappiello et al. (2006).
7 It must be noted that our measure of 'first-order' volatility persistence, which follows Fang and Miller (2009), is not considering the contribution of the lagged error term in the mean equation.
8 Jones et al. (1998) presents a regime-switching GARCH specification which allows the degree of volatility persistence to vary and, hence, may enable us to provide more rigorous interpretations of the volatility persistence issue. We leave the use of their methodology for future research.

9 On the other hand, the coefficients in the conditional mean equation are not significant even at the 10% level. This does not trigger significant concerns, however, because our analysis focuses on the volatility dynamics of bond index returns.

10 In the implementation of the method, we search for up to five breaks and use a trimming parameter of 0.15.

11 In terms of the specification incorporating dummy variables into the conditional mean and variance equations, we referred to the approach used by Fang and Miller (2009).

References

Bai, J., Perron, P. (1998) Estimating and testing linear models with multiple structural changes, *Econometrica*, **66**, 47–78.

Bai, J., Perron, P. (2003) Computation and analysis of multiple structural change models, *Journal of Applied Econometrics*, **18**, 1–22.

Blanco, R., Brennan, S., March, I. W. (2005) An empirical analysis of the dynamic relation between investment-grade bonds and credit default swaps, *Journal of Finance*, **60**, 2255–2281.

Bollerslev, T. (1986) Generalized autoregressive conditional heteroskedasticity, *Journal of Econometrics*, **31**, 307–327.

Cappiello, L., Engle, R. F., Sheppard, K. (2006) Asymmetric dynamics in the correlations of global equity and bond returns, *Journal of Financial Econometrics*, **4**, 537–572.

Cecchetti, S. G., Flores-Lagunes, A., Krause, S. (2006) Assessing the sources of changes in the volatility of real growth, NBER Working Paper no. 11946, National Bureau of Economic Research, Cambridge, MA.

Covarrubias, G., Ewing, B. T., Hein, S. E., Thompson, M. A. (2006) Modeling volatility changes in the 10-year Treasury, *Physica A*, **369**, 737–744.

Cunado J., Biscarri, J. G., Fernando-Perez, G. (2004) Structural changes in volatility and stock market development: evidence for Spain, *Journal of Banking and Finance*, **28**, 1745–1773.

De Goeij, P., Marquering, W. (2004) Modeling the conditional covariance between stock and bond returns: A multivariate GARCH approach, *Journal of Financial Econometrics*, **2**, 531–564.

Delis, M. D., Mylonidis, N. (2011) The chicken or the egg? A note on the dynamic interrelation between government bond spreads and credit default swaps, *Finance Research Letters*, **8**, 163–170.

Fang, W. S., Miller, S. M. (2008) The great moderation and the relationship between output growth and its volatility, *Southern Economic Journal*, **74**, 819–838.

Fang W. S., Miller, S. M. (2009) Modelling the volatility of real GDP growth: the case of Japan revisited, *Japan and World Economy*, **21**, 312–324.

Glosten, L. R., Jagannathan, R., Runkle, D. E. (1993) On the relation between the expected value and the volatility of the nominal excess return on stocks, *Journal of Finance*, **48**, 1779–1801.

Hammoudeh, S., Li, H. (2008) Sudden changes in volatility in emerging markets: the case of Gulf Arab stock markets, *International Review of Financial Analysis*, **17**, 47–63.

Jones, C. M., Lamont, O., Lumsdaine, R. L. (1998) Macroeconomic news and bond market volatility, *Journal of Financial Economics*, **47**, 315–337.

Kasimati, E. (2011) Did the climb on the Greek sovereign spreads cause the devaluation of euro? *Applied Economics Letters*, **18**, 851–854.

Malik, F. (2003) Sudden changes in variance and volatility persistence in foreign exchange markets, *Journal of Multinational Financial Management*, **13**, 217–230.

Malik, F., Ewing, B.T., Payne, J.E. (2005) Measuring volatility persistence in the presence of sudden changes in the variance of Canadian stock returns, *Canadian Journal of Economics*, **38**, 1037–1056.

Nelson, D.B. (1991) Conditional heteroskedasticity in asset returns: a new approach, *Econometrica*, **59**, 347–370.

Oliveira, L., Curto, J.D., Nunes, J.P. (2012) The determinants of sovereign credit spread changes in the Euro-zone, *Journal of International Financial Market, Institutions, and Money*, **22**, 278–304.

Rapach, D.E., Strauss, J.K. (2008) Structural breaks and GARCH models of exchange rate volatility, *Journal of Applied Econometrics*, **23**, 65–90.

Tamakoshi, G. (2011) European sovereign debt crisis and linkage of long-term government bond yields, *Economics Bulletin*, **31**, 2191–203.

Wang, P., Moore, T. (2009) Sudden changes in volatility: the case of five central European stock markets, *Journal of International Financial Markets, Institutions, and Money*, **19**, 33–46.

8 Structural breaks in spillovers among banking stock indices in the EMU

8.1. Introduction

The global credit crisis of 2007–2009, which originated in the US subprime loan market, influenced not only its country of origin, but also the financial system in the European Monetary Union (EMU). As the crisis hit the EMU economy and its banking industry faced a large crash, governments provided capital injections or guarantees for financial sector liabilities and resorted to aggressive fiscal stimulus measures. The resulting fragility of the banking sector became one of the factors used to explain sovereign spreads in the Euro area (Sgherri and Zoli, 2009). After excessive debt issuance, some peripheral countries received negative perceptions by market participants about their fate, resulting in the onset of the sovereign debt crisis in Greece. The problems in Greece also generated fear about heavily indebted countries such as Portugal, Ireland, Italy, and Spain. Thereafter, the EU and IMF agreed on bailout packages for Ireland and Portugal, as well as Greece. That both crises triggered such chain reactions across countries spurred considerable interest in the cross-country spillover effects of shocks or in other words, contagion.

Despite the proliferation of research on contagion effects between equity markets, few studies have focused specifically on spillovers among banking sector stock indices. The banking industry is characterized by its financial intermediary roles. This means that, in addition to affecting other banks, an industry failure may have adverse effects on the entire economy. Further, banks are highly interdependent, owing to their relationships through interbank markets. Such tight relationships transmit risks among banks domestically and across national borders. As Kaufman (1994) contends, the banking sector is more likely to experience contagion than other sectors and contagion triggers serious concern if adverse effects are transmitted to the financial system as a whole. This understanding of the nature of the industry motivated us to investigate the return and volatility spillovers among the banking stock indices of several EMU countries most affected by the financial crises described above.

There has been some research on spillovers between banking sector stock prices. Gropp and Moerman (2003) analysed the weekly first difference of the distance to default[1] for 67 EU banks between 1991 and 2003 and found non-linearity in the tails of the distribution. They thereby proposed a non-parametric measure of contagion among banks and confirmed that the measure appeared sensible for most countries. Then, Gropp et al. (2006) applied a multinomial logit model to stock price data for 50 European banks from January 1994 to January 2003, detecting evidence of cross-country contagion among the banks. More recently, Poirson and Schmittmann (2013) employed a factor approach to analyse stock return data for 83 banks during the period 2002–2011 and found increased sensitivity of the banks to global risk. Their empirical results also indicated that the effects of the European sovereign debt crisis on the banks' sensitivity to global risk were less dominant than the effects of the global credit crisis. These studies focused on the contagion effects among banks at the firm (individual bank) level.

Here, we examine return and volatility transmissions among banking industry stock indices at the country level in seven Euro area countries, namely Greece, Ireland, Portugal, Italy, Spain, Germany, and France, between 1999 and 2011. We believe that our study makes two primary contributions to related literature. First, we are among the first to study spillovers across country banking stock indices by employing the dynamic spillover measure proposed by Diebold and Yilmaz (2012). This methodology builds on the familiar concept of forecast error variance decompositions and is invariant to the order of variables owing to its use of a generalized vector autoregression (VAR) framework[2]. This approach can also provide an economically tractable measure for spillover effects *over time*. This allows us to assess how the spillover effects evolved during the financial crises, which heavily affected the EMU banking sector. Second, our analysis of linkages among banking stock indices at the *country* level may offer complementary insights on a broader level to the current body of knowledge, given that most previous studies focused on the firm level. Here, international investors may be interested in diversifying and managing risk among the stock prices of individual banks but also among country stock indices within the banking sector.

Our empirical results indicate that, on average, a considerable portion of the forecast error variance stems from cross-country spillovers for returns and volatilities among the EMU nations' banking stock indices. We also find that volatility spillovers and return spillovers exhibit strikingly different dynamic behaviour. A rolling-window estimation revealed bursts of volatility spillovers from August 2007 to late 2008, suggesting possible structural breaks during the global credit crisis. The volatility spillovers then fell dramatically after late 2009, even in the wake of the European sovereign debt crisis, partly because the European Central Bank (ECB) took several non-standard measures, injecting massive liquidity into the financial system. In contrast, the return spillovers appeared to be more stable over time, with a gently increasing trend, and remained high even after the sharp increase in September 2009. Moreover, during the sample period, Greece, Ireland, and Portugal were mostly net transmitters of return and volatility spillovers, while Italy and Spain were net receivers. These findings have crucial implications for investors who incorporate spillover effects in their diversification strategies. They are also of importance to policymakers who monitor the degree and direction of spillovers (i.e. from/to a specific country) to maintain the stability of a financial system.

8.2. Empirical methodology

In this study, we use the spillover index advocated by Diebold and Yilmaz (2012), which is based on the concept of variance decomposition. The Diebold and Yilmaz (DY) methodology proceeds as follows. We begin with the following covariance stationary N-variable VAR

$$x_t = \sum_{i=1}^{p} \Phi_i x_{t-i} + \varepsilon_t, \tag{1}$$

where $\varepsilon \sim (0, \Sigma)$ is a vector of disturbances that are independently and identically distributed. The moving average representation of this VAR system is given by $x_t = \sum_{i=0}^{\infty} A_i \varepsilon_{t-i}$, where the matrix A_i is defined as $A_i = \Phi_1 A_{i-1} + ... + \Phi_p A_{i-p}$, with A_0 being an $N \times N$ identity matrix. We employ variance decomposition to evaluate the fraction of the H-step-ahead error variance in forecasting x_i, which is due to shocks to x_j, with $\forall j \neq i$ for each i.

The Cholesky factorization identification scheme would enable us to obtain orthogonal innovations, which are necessary for the calculation of variance decompositions. However, we would then depend on the ordering of the variables. To circumvent this issue, Diebold and Yilmaz (2012) utilized the generalized VAR approach[3], which produces variance decompositions invariant to the ordering of the variables. We define cross variance shares, or 'spillovers', as the fractions of the H-step-ahead error variances in forecasting x_i due to shocks to x_j, for $i, j = 1, 2,..., N$, such that $i \neq j$. The H-step-ahead forecast error variance decomposition is specified as

$$\theta_{ij}^g(H) = \frac{\sigma_{jj}^{-1} \sum_{h=0}^{H-1} (e_i' A_h \Sigma e_j)^2}{\sum_{h=0}^{H-1} (e_i' A_h \Sigma A_h' e_i)}, \tag{2}$$

where Σ is the variance matrix for the error vector, ε, σ_{jj} is the standard deviation of the error term for the jth equation, and e_i is the selection vector, with 1 as the ith element and zero otherwise. To compute the spillover index, we normalize each entry of the variance decomposition matrix by the row sum, such that

$$\tilde{\theta}_{ij}^g(H) = \frac{\theta_{ij}^g(H)}{\sum_{j=1}^{N} \theta_{ij}^g(H)}, \tag{3}$$

with $\sum_{j=1}^{N} \tilde{\theta}_{ij}^{g}(H) = 1$ and $\sum_{i,j=1}^{N} \tilde{\theta}_{ij}^{g}(H) = N$, by construction. Then, we can produce

the 'total spillover index' as follows:

$$S^{g}(H) = 100 \times \frac{\sum_{i,j=1,i \neq j}^{N} \tilde{\theta}_{ij}^{g}(H)}{\sum_{i,j=1}^{N} \tilde{\theta}_{ij}^{g}(H)} = 100 \times \frac{\sum_{i,j=1,i \neq j}^{N} \tilde{\theta}_{ij}^{g}(H)}{N}. \tag{4}$$

The total spillover index allows us to measure the faction of spillovers to the total forecast error variance. A rolling-window estimation in this framework provides the time-varying evolution of spillover effects.

Diebold and Yilmaz (2012) also introduced the concepts of 'directional spillovers' and 'net spillovers'. Directional spillovers signify a decomposition of the total spillovers into those stemming from (or to) a particular market. The directional spillovers received by market i *from* all other markets j are defined as

$$S_{i \leftarrow j}^{g}(H) = 100 \times \frac{\sum_{j=1,j \neq i}^{N} \tilde{\theta}_{ij}^{g}(H)}{\sum_{i,j=1}^{N} \tilde{\theta}_{ij}^{g}(H)} = 100 \times \frac{\sum_{j=1,j \neq i}^{N} \tilde{\theta}_{ij}^{g}(H)}{N}, \tag{5}$$

and similarly, the directional spillovers transmitted by market i *to* all other markets j are written as

$$S_{i \rightarrow j}^{g}(H) = 100 \times \frac{\sum_{j=1,j \neq i}^{N} \tilde{\theta}_{ji}^{g}(H)}{\sum_{i,j=1}^{N} \tilde{\theta}_{ji}^{g}(H)} = 100 \times \frac{\sum_{j=1,j \neq i}^{N} \tilde{\theta}_{ji}^{g}(H)}{N}. \tag{6}$$

Now, net spillovers from market i to all other markets j, which indicate whether a particular market is a net receiver or transmitter of shocks, can be computed by subtracting Equation (5) from Equation (6):

$$S_{i}^{g}(H) = S_{i \rightarrow j}^{g}(H) - S_{i \leftarrow j}^{g}(H). \tag{7}$$

We use these measures in the subsequent analysis of both return and volatility spillovers between the EMU banking sector stock indices.

8.3. Data

Our underlying dataset consists of daily observations from the Datastream banking sector stock indices, with the sample period ranging from 1 January 1990 to 31 December 2011. Our choice of beginning date is constrained by data availability for the seven countries investigated, namely the GIIPS countries (Greece, Ireland, Italy, Portugal, and Spain), Germany, and France, whose banking sectors were severely affected by the recent European financial crises. Weekly Friday-to-Friday returns are calculated as the difference of the logarithm of the stock indices.

Table 8.1 displays the basic statistics for the weekly return data. The mean of the stock index returns takes negative values for all countries. It is notable that the standard deviation is especially large for Ireland, indicating that the recent financial turbulence had a substantially negative impact on the nation's banking sector. The negative value of the skewness for all markets indicates that large decreases are more likely to occur than increases. The high kurtosis suggests the existence of fat tails in the return distribution.

In order to estimate the weekly variance of the stock index returns, we follow the approach advocated by Diebold and Yilmaz (2009), such that

$$\tilde{\sigma}_t^2 = 0.511(H_t - L_t)^2 - 0.019[(C_t - O_t)(H_t + L_t - 2O_t) \\ - 2(H_t - O_t)(L_t - O_t)] - 0.383(C_t - O_t)^2, \tag{8}$$

where Ht is the weekly high, Lt is the weekly low, Ct is the Friday closing, and Ot is the Monday opening (all data are in natural logarithm form). The corresponding estimate of the weekly standard deviation (i.e. volatility) is $\tilde{\sigma}_t$. Note that we do not use GARCH-class models to estimate volatility in order to avoid estimating too many parameters and resorting to a subjective model choice. The descriptive statistics for the estimated weekly volatility data are reported in Table 8.2.

Table 8.1 Summary statistics of the EMU banking stock index return

	GR	IE	PT	IT	ES	DE	FR
Mean	−0.0042	−0.0065	−0.0030	−0.0020	−0.0006	−0.0015	−0.0006
Median	−0.0023	−0.0018	−0.0005	0.0019	0.0012	0.0002	0.0020
Maximum	0.2424	0.4746	0.1690	0.2003	0.1544	0.2797	0.2331
Minimum	−0.2678	−0.6565	−0.1866	−0.2618	−0.2352	−0.4399	−0.2718
Std. Dev.	0.0535	0.0935	0.0353	0.0421	0.0414	0.0487	0.0504
Skewness	−0.3353	−0.6923	−0.6751	−1.0201	−0.7447	−0.8838	−0.4230
Kurtosis	5.9322	14.7630	7.5861	9.6255	7.8014	17.1348	7.6052

Table 8.2 Summary statistics of the EMU banking stock index volatility

	GR	IE	PT	IT	ES	DE	FR
Mean	0.0220	0.0301	0.0130	0.0164	0.0170	0.0180	0.0204
Median	0.0171	0.0176	0.0094	0.0126	0.0136	0.0143	0.0153
Maximum	0.1332	0.3364	0.0917	0.1040	0.0853	0.1115	0.1183
Minimum	0.0010	0.0010	0.0005	0.0001	0.0008	0.0011	0.0007
Std. Dev.	0.0169	0.0357	0.0117	0.0133	0.0125	0.0149	0.0161
Skewness	2.1961	3.3751	2.1583	2.2157	1.8638	2.7542	2.1086
Kurtosis	10.1177	19.4962	10.0259	9.8648	7.7274	14.0904	9.2041

8.4. Empirical results

Spillover tables

Table 8.3 shows the spillover indices for returns over the entire sample. The results are based on VAR of order 2 selected using the BIC with generalized variance decompositions of 10-day-ahead forecast errors. The *ij*th entry in the table represents the estimated contribution to the forecast error variance of country *i* stemming from innovations to country *j*. The value of the total spillover index indicates that, on average, 67.6% of the return forecast error variance results from spillovers, suggesting a high level of interdependence in the EMU banking sector stock markets. It is worth mentioning that Spain, Italy, France, and Germany take relatively higher values of both 'Directional to others' spillovers and 'Directional from others' spillovers. This result implies that factors such as the openness of the financial market or the banking sector matter when determining the extent to which the country of interest transmits or receives return spillovers. Table 8.4 presents the spillover indices for volatility. These results are also based on VAR of order 2 selected using the BIC. Here again, we detect quite a high value of the total spillover index (59.7%). This suggests that a substantial portion of the forecast error variance is explained by volatility spillovers, highlighting the importance of volatility transmission across the EMU banking sector stock markets.

Spillover plots

Tables 8.3 and 8.4 provide useful information on the 'average' return and volatility spillovers over the full sample. Nonetheless, we are also interested in how return and volatility spillovers evolve over time, especially since our sample includes the crisis periods, which must have triggered changes in

Table 8.3 Spillover table of the EMU banking stock index return

| To (i) | From (j) | | | | | | | Directional |
	GR	IE	PT	IT	ES	DE	FR	from others
GR	41.8	8.2	8.5	10.3	11.3	10.1	9.8	58.2
IE	7.4	39.0	7.6	11.5	12.4	9.7	12.5	61.1
PT	7.2	7.0	37.0	12.9	13.4	10.9	11.5	62.9
IT	6.4	7.7	9.5	26.5	18.0	15.4	16.5	73.5
ES	7.1	8.3	9.9	18.0	26.4	14.5	15.9	73.7
DE	6.3	6.8	8.6	16.6	15.7	28.8	17.3	71.3
FR	6.5	8.8	8.4	16.9	16.2	15.9	27.3	72.7
Directional to others	40.9	46.8	52.5	86.2	87.0	76.5	83.5	Total spillover index
Directional including own	82.7	85.8	89.5	112.7	113.4	105.3	110.8	= 67.6%

Table 8.4 Spillover table of the EMU banking stock index volatility

| To (i) | From (j) | | | | | | | Directional |
	GR	IE	PT	IT	ES	DE	FR	from others
GR	53.4	5.1	7.6	12.5	6.7	6.1	8.6	46.6
IE	5.2	49.6	7.2	9.2	9.1	10.2	9.4	50.3
PT	8.8	4.6	43.7	13.9	10.6	6.6	11.8	56.3
IT	6.2	5.3	8.4	33.1	17.2	13.3	16.5	66.9
ES	4.5	5.8	7.2	17.9	35.3	14.0	15.4	64.8
DE	3.7	7.1	4.4	16.6	15.9	35.5	16.8	64.5
FR	5.9	5.2	6.7	18.2	18.4	14.2	31.4	68.6
Directional to others	34.3	33.1	41.5	88.3	77.9	64.4	78.5	Total spillover index
Directional including own	87.7	82.7	85.2	121.4	113.2	99.9	109.9	= 59.7%

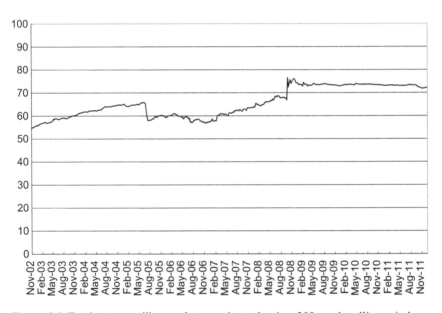

Figure 8.1 Total return spillover plot – estimated using 200-week rolling windows (in percentage)

spillover behaviour among the banking stock indices. Hence, we estimate return and volatility spillovers using 200-week rolling samples[4], resulting in the total return and volatility spillover plots in Figure 8.1 and Figure 8.2, respectively. Comparing these two figures provides us with the following three main insights.

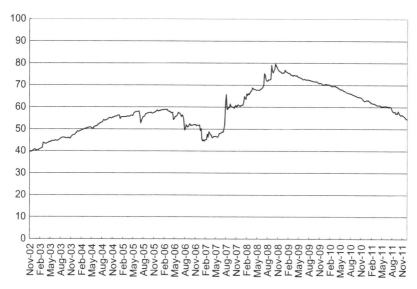

Figure 8.2 Total volatility spillover plot – estimated using 200-week rolling windows (in percentage)

First, the return spillover plot generally displays more stable behaviour than that of the volatility plot until its hike in September 2008, with the collapse of Lehman Brothers. The gradually increasing trend of the time-varying return spillovers may reflect the sustained financial integration and interconnectedness of banks in the Euro area. Such relatively tranquil paths of return spillovers during pre-crisis periods are generally consistent with findings by previous studies using the spillover index. These studies include Diebold and Yilmaz (2009) (on 19 stock market indices, including both developed and emerging countries) and Yilmaz (2010) (on stock market indices in 10 east Asian countries).

Second, the volatility spillover plot generally exhibits larger variability, especially during the recent financial turbulences. Indeed, it reached a peak in August 2007, when the global credit crunch effectively began in the US subprime loan market, triggered by BNP Paribas's liquidation of two funds heavily invested in mortgage back securities. In contrast, the return spillover plot was almost uneventful at that time. During the periods between August 2007 and September 2009, other hikes of volatility spillovers were observed. These observations indicate that the evolution of the volatility spillover index for the EMU banking stock indices was very responsive to economic events symbolizing the global credit crisis. In particular, our empirical results imply that August 2007, which is usually interpreted as the onset of the global credit crunch, was also an important structural break point for the EMU banking stock markets, as reflected by the burst of volatility spillovers.

Third, since early 2009, the volatility spillover plot reveals a markedly decreasing trend, while the return spillover plot remains very high, between 70% and 75%. This pattern of the volatility spillover index continued, even during the recent European sovereign debt crisis. For instance, events such as the Greek government's revision of its public deficit in November 2009 and Greece's bailout application to the EU and the IMF in April 2010 did not generate any volatility spillover hikes. In fact, from late 2008 until the end of 2011, the ECB implemented a series of unconventional monetary policies to boost the liquidity of the markets in the wake of the financial distress. These policies included a fixed-rate tender procedure with full allotment for carrying out all weekly main refinancing operations on 8 October 2008, the Securities Markets Programme to purchase sovereign bonds of affected countries on 9 May 2010, and the three-year long-term refinancing operations on 8 December 2011. The gradual decline in volatility spillovers during that period suggests that such non-standard measures may have been important in calming the contagion among the banking stock indices of the EMU nations, despite the emergence of the sovereign debt crisis.

Next, we investigate the 'net spillovers' for each of the seven countries. Net spillovers are defined as the difference between the directional spillovers by the country transmitted to and received from all other markets. Studying the net spillovers helps us to identify which countries were transmitters (in the case of positive values) or receivers (in the case of negative values) of shocks in net terms at each point in time. Figure 8.3 presents the net return spillovers over time. From this graph, we can see that Greece, Ireland, and Portugal were mostly net receivers of shocks in the banking sector stock returns, while Italy, Spain, Germany, and France were net transmitters. This may be due to the relatively large size of the banking industry (measured by such indicators as total assets and total loans) in the latter four countries. Figure 8.4, which reports time-varying net volatility spillovers, exhibits a slightly different picture, with a higher degree of variability and heterogeneity of time-varying patterns across markets than shown in Figure 8.3. According to Figure 8.4, in terms of volatility spillovers, Greece, Ireland, and Portugal were net receivers, while Italy and Spain were net transmitters for most periods. Nonetheless, it is worth noting that Ireland was a net transmitter of volatility shocks from mid-2007 to early 2009, implying that the financial distress in the banking sector led the country to become a possible source of volatility transmission during the global financial crisis period. Another interesting observation from Figure 8.4 is that France made a transition from being a net transmitter to a net receiver of volatility shocks in late 2008. This suggests that the country should become more aware of the potential propagation of shocks originating from the recent uncertainty in banking sector stocks in other EMU countries.

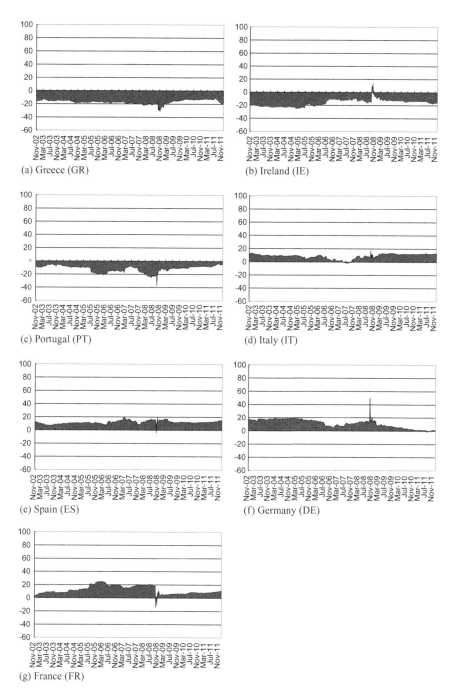

Figure 8.3 Net return spillovers – estimated using 200-week rolling windows (in percentage)

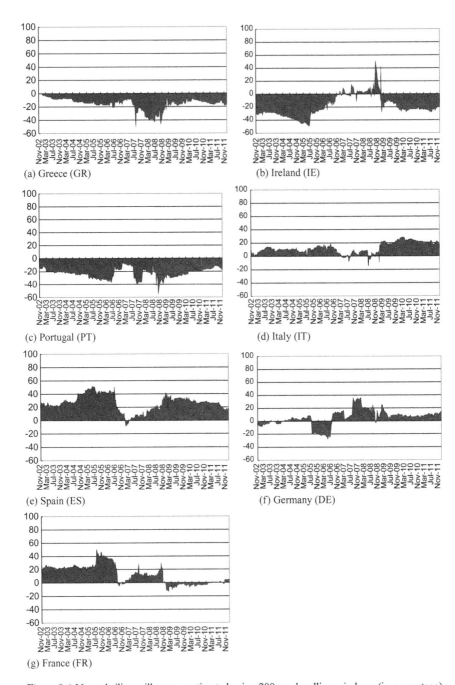

Figure 8.4 Net volatility spillovers – estimated using 200-week rolling windows (in percentage)

8.5. Conclusion

In the present study, we examined return and volatility spillovers among banking sector stock indices in seven EMU countries (Greece, Ireland, Portugal, Italy, Spain, Germany, and France) between 1999 and 2011. We employed the spillover measure developed by Diebold and Yilmaz (2012) based on the generalized VAR framework, which is invariant to variable ordering. Using this approach, we derived a single spillover index distilling all cross-country spillover effects from the well-known concept of forecast error variances. Further, we used a rolling-window estimation within this framework to display the time-varying path of spillovers for returns and volatilities.

The main findings from our empirical analysis are as follows. 1) The total spillover index measures indicate that substantial portions of forecast error variances stem from spillovers, both for the returns (67.6%) and volatilities (59.7%), on average, over the sample period. 2) The total spillover plot for returns exhibits a gradually increasing trend prior to the bankruptcy of Lehman Brothers and is relatively stable after that, indicating that the integration of the financial markets and the banking sectors in the EMU was maintained. 3) The volatility spillover plot is more volatile and exhibits bursts that coincide with various crisis events that took place during the global credit crunch, when regime switches in the volatility spillovers may have occurred. 4) However, the volatility spillover plot decreases substantially after early 2009, despite the onset of the European sovereign debt crisis, presumably owing to several unconventional policies implemented by the ECB to improve liquidity conditions. 5) Throughout the sample period, Italy and Spain were dominant net transmitters of both return and volatility spillovers, while Greece, Ireland, and Portugal were net receivers. Importantly, this pattern is not a result of the recent debt crisis. 6) However, Ireland transmitted volatility shocks to other countries in net terms, especially during the 2007–2009 global credit crisis.

Our empirical results are relevant for both international investors and policymakers. Investors can exploit the knowledge on cross-country return and volatility spillover effects in formulating diversification strategies. Specifically, the information on the identified spillovers is useful for executing timely risk management for portfolios with a certain level of exposure to banking industry stock indices. Then, the spillover measure among the indices can serve as a helpful monitoring tool for policymakers in the EMU in maintaining the smooth functioning of the banking system. In particular, policymakers in Greece, Ireland, and Portugal, countries that have historically been at the receiving end of return and volatility spillovers, should try to prevent spillover effects from the banking sector stock indices in other countries.

Notes

1 According to Gropp and Moerman (2003), default to distance is defined as the number of standard deviations away from the default point where the liabilities of the bank are equal to its assets.

2 The Diebold and Yilmaz (2012) method contrasts sharply with that of Diebold and Yilmaz (2009), which employs Cholesky-factor identification and thus depends on the order of variables in the VAR system.

3 See Koop et al. (1996) and Pesaran and Shin (1998) for details of the generalized VAR method.
4 We also employed 100-week rolling samples and confirmed that the total return and volatility spillover plots looked qualitatively similar. We do not report the results here.

References

Diebold, F. X., Yilmaz, K. (2009) Measuring financial asset return and volatility spillovers, with application to global equity markets, *Economic Journal*, **119**, 158–171.

Diebold, F. X., Yilmaz, K. (2012) Better to give than to receive: Predictive directional measurement of volatility spillovers, *International Journal of Forecasting*, **28**, 57–66.

Gropp, R., Moerman, G. (2003) Measurement of contagion in banks' equity prices, ECB Working Paper no. 297, European Central Bank, Frankfurt.

Gropp, R., Duca, M. L., Vesala, J. (2006) Cross-border bank contagion in Europe, ECB Working Paper no. 662, European Central Bank, Frankfurt.

Kaufman, G. (1994) Bank contagion: A review of the theory and evidence, *Journal of Financial Services Research*, **8**, 123–150.

Koop, G., Pesaran, M. H., Potter, S. M. (1996) Impulse response analysis in nonlinear multivariate models, *Journal of Econometrics*, **74**, 119–147.

Pesaran, M. H., Shin, Y. (1998) Generalized impulse response analysis in linear multivariate models, *Economic Letters*, **58**, 17–29.

Poirson, H., Schmittmann, J. (2013) Risk exposures and financial spillovers in tranquil and crisis times: Bank-level evidence, IMF Working Paper no. 13/142, International Monetary Fund, Washington, DC.

Sgherri, S., Zoli, E. (2009) Euro area sovereign risk during the crisis, IMF Working Paper no. 09/222, International Monetary Fund, Washington, DC.

Yilmaz, K. (2010) Return and volatility spillovers among the East Asian equity markets, *Journal of Asian Economics*, **21**, 304–313.

9 Structural breaks in the relationship between the Eonia and Euribor rates

9.1. Introduction

In this chapter, we analyse the relationship between two important short-term interbank interest rates offered by European banks—the Eonia rate (EON) and the 3-month Euribor rate (ER3). EON, the overnight rate regarded as the operational target of the ECB, not only contains information on market expectations about the monetary policy stance in the near future but also anchors interest rates with longer maturities. Euribor rates are said to provide preeminent interest rates for various financial products, including interest rate swaps and futures. Among Euribor rates, ER3 is used throughout the study, because the 3-month maturity has been the focus of recent empirical studies of financial crises in interbank money markets. Understanding the dynamics between the two rates is of critical importance for efficient implementation of monetary policy by the ECB, because one of its main goals is to influence the very short-term interest rates in the interbank money market, as Hassler and Nautz (2008) point out.

A number of researchers have studied the linkage between the overnight federal funds rate and US Treasury bills (e.g. Cook and Hahn, 1989; Rudebusch, 1995, Woodford, 1999, Sarno and Thornton, 2003; Thornton, 2005). These authors insist that the co-movement of these rates may be driven by the expectations hypothesis of the term structure of the interest rates, which states that longer-term interest rates are determined by market expectations of shorter-term interest rates and a constant risk premium. Compared to these studies, which focused on the US financial market, only a few have investigated the relationship between the overnight rate and the short-term interest rates in the context of monetary policy in the euro area. Nautz and Offermanns (2007) show that the reaction of the Eonia rate to the term spread (the 3-month Euribor minus the Eonia) is not symmetric (i.e. it relies on the directions of expected interest rate changes). They also find that the dynamics between the Eonia and the term spread depends on the applied repo auction format. Cossetti and Guidi (2009) examine the long-run relationship between the Eonia and Euro area interest rates with several maturities and find that cointegration was rejected for maturities longer than 6 years, suggesting that ECB's actions may not have a significant impact on the entire yield curve.

The methodology used here is in line with recent empirical studies on the dynamic relationship between interest rates that may be characterized by asymmetry (Sarno and Thornton, 2003; Nautz and Offermanns, 2007). To our knowledge, this study is among the first to use the two-regime threshold cointegration approach advocated by Hansen and Seo (2002) to analyse the linkage between short-term interest rates. This method considers the possibility that short-run dynamics are characterized by different regimes, based on a threshold. Using monthly data on EON and ER3 from January 1999 to December 2011, we find evidence supporting the existence of threshold cointegration. In addition, it is only in an 'extreme' regime where ER3 increases relative to EON that error correlation takes place through an adjustment of ER3, as the expectations hypothesis anticipates. This regime corresponds to the periods when the interbank market tensions were high, in particular with the deterioration of the recent financial turmoil (the European sovereign debt crisis as well as the global financial crisis) and thus the ECB took bold measures to alleviate them.

The rest of the chapter is organized as follows. Section 9.2 briefly describes the empirical methodology. Section 9.3 describes the data used. Section 9.4 discusses the results of our analysis, and Section 9.5 concludes.

9.2. Empirical methodology

We employ the threshold cointegration approach proposed by Hansen and Seo (2002). While a traditional, linear vector error correction model (VECM) assumes a constant speed of adjustment towards a long-run equilibrium, threshold cointegration approaches hold that error correction occurs depending on a threshold. Earlier studies on testing for threshold cointegration (e.g. Balke and Fomby, 1997; Lo and Zivot, 2001)[1] assume that the cointegration vector is known. Unlike those approaches, Hansen and Seo's (2002) methodology is unique in that it considers a case where the cointegration vector is unknown and, therefore, is estimated from the data.

Specifically, these authors consider a two-regime threshold cointegration model, which can be regarded as a nonlinear VECM of order $l + 1$ as follows:

$$\Delta x_t = \begin{cases} A_1' X_{t-1}(\beta) + u_t & if \quad w_{t-1}(\beta) \leq \gamma \\ A_2' X_{t-1}(\beta) + u_t & if \quad w_{t-1}(\beta) > \gamma \end{cases}, \tag{1}$$

with

$$X_{t-1}' = (1, w_{t-1}(\beta), \Delta x_{t-1}, ..., \Delta x_{t-l}),$$

where $w_t(\beta) = \beta x_t$ is the I(0) error correction term, x_t is a I(1) time series with one cointegrating vector β, A_1 and A_2 are coefficient matrices describing the dynamics in each regime, γ is the threshold parameter, and u_t is an error term. In this study, x_t corresponds to [ER3$_t$,EON$_t$], as we investigate the bivariate case of asymmetric transmission between ER3$_t$ and EON$_t$. As can be seen in (1), this model has two regimes, and the error-correction mechanism differs depending on deviations from the equilibrium below or above the threshold parameter γ.

Our test will compare the null hypothesis of linear cointegration (that no threshold effect exists) with the alternative hypothesis of threshold cointegration, as represented by model (1). Here, we use the heteroskedastic consistent Lagrange Multiplier (*sup LM*) test developed by Hansen and Seo (2002), denoted by

$$sup\ LM = \sup_{\gamma_L \leq \gamma \leq \gamma_U} LM\ (\tilde{\beta}, \gamma), \tag{2}$$

where $\tilde{\beta}$ is the null hypothesis estimate of β, and $[\gamma_L, \gamma_U]$ is the search region determined so that γ_L is the π_0-th percentile of $\tilde{w}_{t-1}$ and γ_U is the $(1 - \pi_0)$-th percentile of $\tilde{w}_{t-1}^2$. Then, the two bootstrap methods, namely the fixed regressor bootstrap and the residual bootstrap, are employed to calculate *p*-values with 5,000 simulations.

9.3. Data

Our monthly dataset on EON and ER3 is sourced from the ECB Statistical Data Warehouse. The data cover the period from January 1999, when the euro was introduced, to December 2011. Eonia is the interest rate calculated by the ECB as an average of all unsecured lending rates in the overnight interbank market, published daily by Reuters. A Euribor rate is the rate at which European banks borrow funds from each other. The rate depends not only on demand and supply but also on external factors such as inflation and economic growth. More than 50 European banks with high credit ratings and money market volume form the Euribor as well as the Eonia panels. As Figure 9.1 indicates, EON and ER3 moved together. Nevertheless, the rates tended to diverge frequently during the global financial crisis that originated in the US subprime loan market in August

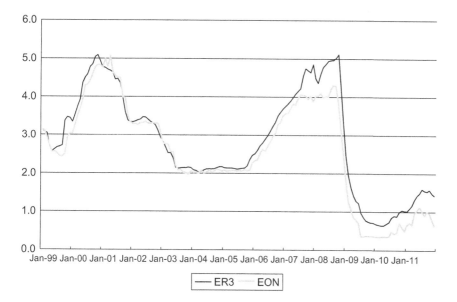

Figure 9.1 Historical paths of the Eonia rate (EON) and the 3-month Euribor rate (ER3)

Table 9.1 Unit root tests

	ADF test		PP test	
	Level	First differences	Level	First differences
ER3	−1.7663	−5.6694***	−1.5529	−5.6062***
EON	−1.5788	−4.3958***	−1.2794	−7.8046***

*** denotes statistical significance at the 1% level.

2007 and in the second half of 2011 when the European sovereign debt crisis intensified, with an increased strain on the banking sector in the area.

We conduct the ADF test and the Phillips–Perron test to assess the stationarity of each variable. As reported in Table 9.1, we find that both series are first-order integrated and hence validate our use of the cointegration test.

9.4.   Empirical results

We conduct the sup *LM* test as done by Hansen and Seo (2002) to assess the evidence on threshold cointegration. This study selects a lag length of $l = 1$ based on the Akaike Information Criterion (AIC) and the BIC. Table 9.2 presents the test results for the linear versus nonlinear hypothesis with the threshold effect. Our results, based on the Lagrange Multiplier threshold test, clearly reject the null hypothesis of linear cointegration at the 1% significance level with a test statistic of 27.6327, meaning that the threshold cointegration model is more appropriate for our series. Moreover, a Wald test rejects the null hypothesis that the coefficients of error correction terms in both regimes are equal. The

Table 9.2 Tests for threshold cointegration between the Eonia rate and the 3-month Euribor rate

Estimates	Lag = 1
Threshold parameter estimate (γ)	0.7938
Cointegrating vector estimate (β)	0.9174
Lagrange multiplier threshold test	
sup *LM* value	27.6327
Fixed regressor bootstrap *p*-value	0.0010
Residual bootstrap *p*-value	0.0004
Wald test	
p-value for equality of dynamic coefficients	0.0000
p-value for equality of ECM coefficients	0.0000

Note: The selection of a lag length of 1 is based on the AIC and BIC criteria.

Table 9.3 Threshold VECM estimation between the Eonia rate and the 3-month Euribor rate

	Regime 1: $w_{t-1} \leq 0.7938$			
	Percentage of observations = 0.8896			
Dependent variable	$\Delta ER3_t$		ΔEON_t	
Explanatory variable	Estimate	SE	Estimate	SE
Δw_{t-1}	0.0618	0.0482	0.2467***	0.0616
Constant	−0.0136	0.0178	−0.0938***	0.0244
ΔBR_{t-1}	0.5218***	0.0870	0.6087***	0.1164
ΔMR_{t-1}	0.1166	0.0769	−0.1377	0.1017
	Regime 2: $w_{t-1} > 0.7938$			
	Percentage of observations = 0.1104			
Dependent variable	$\Delta ER3_t$		ΔEON_t	
Explanatory variable	Estimate	SE	Estimate	SE
Δw_{t-1}	−0.6970***	0.1037	−0.1185	0.2414
Constant	0.7529***	0.0964	0.0772	0.2618
ΔBR_{t-1}	0.1191	0.1004	0.2746	0.1963
ΔMR_{t-1}	0.9983***	0.1751	0.5799**	0.2809

Note: Eicker–White standard errors are shown in the 'SE' column.

*** and ** denote statistical significance at the 1% and 5% level, respectively.

cointegrating vector and the threshold parameter estimates $(\hat{\beta}, \hat{\gamma})$ are calculated as (0.9174, 0.7938) by a 300 × 300 grid search procedure. This implies that our threshold VECM is partitioned into Regimes 1 and 2. Regime 1, which corresponds to $ER3_{t-1} - 0.91741EON_{t-1} \leq 0.7938\%$, consists of 88.96% of all observations in the sample and, thus, can be referred to as a 'typical' regime. This occurs when ER3 decreases relative to EON. In contrast, Regime 2 is characterized by $| ER3_{t-1} - 0.91741EON_{t-1} |> 0.7938\%$. This takes place when ER3 increases relative to EON and is regarded as an 'extreme' regime in the sense that it comprises only 11.04% of all observations.

Table 9.3 reports the estimation result of the threshold VECM. In the 'typical' regime (Regime 1), the lagged error correction term (the parameter accompanying Δw_{t-1}) is significant at the 1% level only for the equation involving EON. This suggests that error correction in this regime is based only on EON adjustment. Figure 9.2 depicts the response function for the discrepancy between ER3 and the adjustment for the EON in the previous period. It can be seen that on the left-hand side of the threshold parameter, long-run equilibrium adjustments tend to take place through movements of EON rather than ER3. This finding

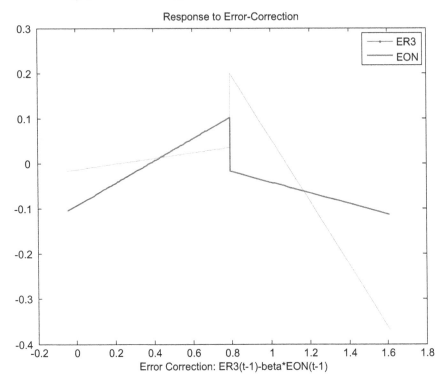

Figure 9.2 Response of the Eonia rate (EON) and the 3-month Euribor rate (ER3) to
          error correlation

seems to be at odds with the expectations hypothesis that EON, which is often
seen as a proxy for the ECB's monetary policy instrument, anchors European
money market interest rates such as ER3. Nonetheless, if the market can correctly
anticipate changes in EON, ER3 might move towards the expected level before
any actual movement in EON, creating the impression that EON is adjusting to
ER3. In fact, Sarno and Thornton (2003), who investigate the dynamic relationship between the US federal funds rate and the Treasury bill, find that the federal
funds rate bears the burden of adjustment towards long-run equilibriums.

Conversely, in the 'extreme' regime (Regime 2), the lagged error correction
term is significant at the 1% level only for the ER3 equation, indicating that
error correlation occurs through the adjustment of ER3 towards a long-run equilibrium. The negative sign of the lagged error correction term indicates that ER3
will decline if its discrepancy with EON is above the equilibrium level. Figure 9.2
shows that on the right-hand side of the threshold parameter, the adjustment
indeed occurs through movements of ER3. Comparing the absolute values of
the estimated error correction terms in both regimes, we find that the adjustment
towards a long-run equilibrium is faster in Regime 2. It has been contended that
the ECB influences short-term interest rates such as ER3 by controlling EON,

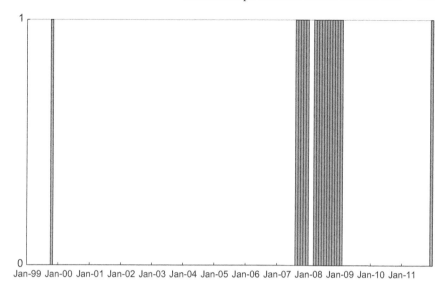

Figure 9.3 Timing of the 'extreme' regime (Regime 2) derived from threshold VECM estimation (shaded area)

which is targeted towards the main refinancing operation and, hence, should move in close proximity to it. In light of this, one might expect that ER3 would adjust to EON. A key implication of our results is that the response of ER3 to a long-run equilibrium is regime dependent; that is, it occurs only in an 'extreme' regime, when ER3 increases relative to EON.

The shaded areas in Figure 9.3 correspond to the periods defined as the 'extreme' regime, where error correction relies on the adjustment of ER3 and not on EON. Clearly, Regime 2 was prevalent between August 2007 and January 2009 and, further, in December 2011. Immediately after the onset of the global financial crisis in August 2007[3], tensions arose in the interbank market as banks became sceptical about the creditworthiness of their counterparties, as mentioned by Cour-Thimann and Winkler (2013). We witnessed the ECB providing an unlimited supply of overnight liquidity to banks as a countermeasure against the crisis. On the other hand, as the European sovereign debt crisis hit Italy and Spain in mid-2011 and investors began having concerns about losses that banks would encounter on their government holdings, the 3-month euro LIBOR-OIS spread, which is an indicator of money market strain, widened sharply, reaching a peak in December 2011 (Allen and Moessner, 2012). In response to this, on 8 December 2011, the ECB announced an unprecedented measure to implement 3-year refinancing operations, where it provided sufficient liquidity over the medium term to banks. With the interbank market turbulence triggered by these crises, the changes in EON itself were unexpected during this 'extreme' regime. Therefore, the short-run responses might have been driven by the adjustment of ER3 rather than EON, as the expectations hypothesis predicts.

9.5.   Conclusion

This chapter examined the dynamic relationship between two key European short-term interest rates, EON and ER3, during January 1999 to December 2011. We used the threshold VECM approach used by Hansen and Seo (2002), which allows for nonlinear adjustments to a long-run equilibrium, to test for the presence of threshold cointegration. Our modelling strategy was motivated by a recent strand of empirical literature showing that dynamic relationships between short-term interest rates may be characterized by asymmetric behaviour.

The main results of our empirical analysis are summarized as follows: 1) Linear cointegration between EON and ER3 is rejected in favour of a two-regime threshold cointegration model with the threshold parameter. 2) In a 'typical' regime, where ER3 decreases relative to EON, error correction is driven only through the adjustment of EON, contrary to the conventional view of the expectations hypothesis in which error correlation occurs through an adjustment of ER3. 3) In contrast, ER3 responds to a long-run equilibrium only in an 'extreme' regime, where it increases relative to EON. 4) Such an 'extreme' regime corresponds to the period of the global financial crisis (particularly between August 2007 to January 2009) and the period of the intensified European debt crisis (in December 2011), when the market could not easily anticipate changes in EON. Our findings on these complex relationships between EON and ER3, including the presence of regime shifts, may be especially helpful for policymakers who need to not only predict potential impacts of a particular policy on market participants but also evaluate the efficacy of monetary policy to influence the very short-term interest rates in the interbank money market, ex post.

Notes

1 Contending that the tendency to move towards a long-run equilibrium may not necessarily occur in every period, Balke and Fomby (1997) propose univariate threshold cointegration models where a known cointegration vector is assumed. Lo and Zivot (2001) extend Balke and Fomby's model to the multivariate case.
2 Andrews (1993) proposes that π_0 lies between 0.05 and 0.15. We assumed that $\pi_0 = 0.05$.
3 On August 9, 2007, BNP Paribas stunned the market by suspending its funds affected by exposures to subprime mortgage liabilities. This event is often regarded as a trigger for the global financial crisis.

References

Allen, W.A., Moessner, R. (2012) The liquidity consequences of the euro area sovereign debt crisis, BIS Working Paper no. 390, Bank for International Settlements, Basel.

Andrews, D.W.K. (1993) Tests for parameter instability and structural change with unknown change point, *Econometrica*, **61**, 821–856.

Balke, N.S., Fomby, T.B. (1997) Threshold cointegration, *International Economic Review*, **38**, 627–645.

Cook, T., Hahn, T. (1989) The effect of change in the federal funds rate target on market interest rates in the 1970s, *Journal of Monetary Economics,* **24**, 331–352.

Cossetti, F., Guidi, F. (2009) ECB monetary policy and term structure of interest rates in the Euro area: an empirical analysis. Working Paper no. 334, Universita' Politecnica delle Marche (I), Dipartimento di Scienze Economiche e Sociali.

Cour-Thimann, P., Winkler, B. (2013) The ECB's non-standard monetary policy measures. The role of institutional factors and financial structure, ECB Working Paper no. 1528, European Central Bank, Frankfurt.

Hansen, B.E., Seo, B. (2002) Testing for two-regime threshold cointegration in vector error-correction models, *Journal of Econometrics*, **110**, 293–318.

Hassler, U., Nautz, D. (2008) On the persistence of the Eonia spread, *Economic Letters*, **101**, 184–187.

Lo, M., Zivot, E. (2001) Threshold cointegration and nonlinear adjustment to the law of one price, *Macroeconmic Dynamics,* **5**, 533–576.

Nautz, D., Offermanns, C.J. (2007) The dynamic relationship between the Euro overnight rate, the ECB's policy rate and the term spread, *International Journal of Finance and Economics*, **12**, 287–300.

Rudebusch, G.D. (1995) Federal reserve interest rate, targeting rational expectations, and the term structure, *Journal of Monetary Economics*, **35**, 245–274.

Sarno, L., Thornton, D.L. (2003) The dynamic relationship between the federal funds rate and the Treasury bill rate: an empirical investigation, *Journal of Banking & Finance*, **27**, 1079–1110.

Thornton, D.L. (2005) Tests of the expectations hypothesis: resolving the anomalies when the short-term is the federal funds rate, *Journal of Banking & finance*, **29**, 2541–2556.

Woodford, M. (1999) Optimal monetary policy inertia. *The Manchester School*, **67** (supplement), 1–35.

First publication of each chapter

Chapter 1 Co-movements among stock markets of European financial institutions

Tamakoshi, G., Hamori, S. (2013) An asymmetric dynamic conditional correlation analysis of linkages of European financial institutions during the Greek sovereign debt crisis, *European Journal of Finance*, **19**, 939–950.

Chapter 2 Co-movements among GIIPS national stock indices

Unpublished article.

Chapter 3 Co-movements among European exchange rates

Tamakoshi, G., Hamori, S. (2014) Co-movements among major European exchange rates: A multivariate time-varying asymmetric approach, *International Review of Economics and Finance*, **31**, 105–113.

Chapter 4 The causality between Greek sovereign bond yields and southern European banking sector equity returns

Tamakoshi G., Hamori, S., (2014) Causality-in-variance and causality-in-mean between the Greek sovereign bond yields and Southern European banking sector equity returns, *Journal of Economics and Finance*, **38**, 627–642.

Chapter 5 Causality between the US dollar and the euro LIBOR-OIS spreads

Tamakoshi, G., Hamori, S., (2014) On cross-currency transmissions between US dollar and euro LIBOR-OIS spreads, *Research in International Business and Finance*, **30**, 83–90.

Chapter 6 Causality between the Euro and Greek sovereign CDS spreads

Unpublished article.

Chapter 7 Structural breaks in the volatility of the Greek sovereign bond index

Tamakoshi, G., Hamori, S. (2014) Greek sovereign bond index, volatility, and structural breaks, *Journal of Economics and Finance*, **38**, 687–697.

Chapter 8 Structural breaks in spillovers among banking stock indices in the EMU

Unpublished article.

Chapter 9 Structural breaks in the relationship between the Eonia and Euribor rates

Tamakoshi G., Hamori, S. (2014) Nonlinear adjustment between the Eonia and Euribor rates: a two-regime threshold cointegration analysis, *Applied Financial Economics*, **24**, 139–143.

Index

Akaike Information Criterion (AIC)
  87, 124
asymmetric DCC (A-DCC) 4, 26, 38
Augmented Dickey–Fuller (ADF) test 15,
  29, 42, 60, 74, 87, 98, 124
autoregressive conditional
  heteroskedasticity (ARCH) 56
autoregressive (AR) model 3, 20, 31, 46

bailout package 1, 11, 29, 41, 49, 82, 108
banking sector 2, 4, 6, 11, 55, 108, 124

causality-in-mean 4, 5, 56, 72
causality-in-variance 5, 37, 56, 71
common currency 34
common factor 17, 43, 68
contagion 2–6, 12, 25, 108
contemporaneous correlation 43
convergence trade hypothesis 2
corporate–government bond spread 4,
  27, 34
Credit Default Swap (CDS) 5, 82
credit risk 5, 11, 71–72, 79, 82, 91
cross-correlation function 4, 5, 37, 56
currency portfolio rebalancing 38, 44
current account deficit 11

dependence structure 38
diversification 3–4, 6, 13, 22, 25, 34, 37,
  48, 109, 119
dummy variable 3, 6, 14, 20, 31, 40,
  46, 104
Dynamic Conditional Correlation (DCC)
  3, 12, 14, 26
Dynamic Equicorrelation (DECO) 3, 25

Eonia rate 6, 121
error correction term 122, 124–126
Euribor rate 6, 121, 123
European Banking Authority 11, 55

European Central Bank (ECB) 5, 79, 101,
  109, 121
European Financial Stability Facility
  (EFSF) 11
European Monetary Union (EMU) 1, 6,
  11, 25, 108
European sovereign debt crisis (Greek
  sovereign debt crisis) 1–4, 6–7, 11, 26,
  55, 72, 82, 98, 109, 122
expectations hypothesis 7, 121
exponential general autoregressive
  conditional heteroskedasticity
  (EGARCH) 27, 57, 74, 98

fiscal imbalance 11
fixed-rate tender procedure 79, 116
fixed regressor bootstrap 123
forecast error variance 6, 109
foreign exchange market intervention 4, 48

generalized autoregressive conditional
  heteroskedasticity (GARCH) 13, 25, 39,
  56, 72, 83, 99, 112
generalized error distribution (GED) 13,
  27, 39, 75
generalized impulse response function
  (G-IRF) 5, 84
GIIPS 1–3, 6, 25, 83, 111
global financial crisis (global subprime
  loan crisis; global credit crisis) 1, 3–5,
  7, 12, 26, 40, 71, 108, 122
global risk aversion 4, 27
Granger causality 5, 58, 84

herd behaviour 32

IMF 1, 29, 41, 82, 108
information flow 5, 56, 78
interbank (money) market 5, 7, 71,
  108, 121

Jarque–Bera tests 15, 29, 42, 60, 74, 87, 98

Lag-augmented VAR (LA-VAR) 5, 83
LIBOR (London Interbank Offer Rate) 5, 71, 85
LIBOR-OIS spread 5, 71, 127
liquidity tension 77
log-likelihood function 28
long-term refinancing operations (LTROs) 80, 116
Ljung–Box statistics 17, 29, 42, 60, 77, 100

Maastricht convergence bond yield 32, 59
Maastricht Treaty 1
macroeconomic fundamental 2, 11
main refinancing operation (MRO) 116, 127
Modified Schwarz Information Criterion (LWZ) 101
monetary policy 121
Morgan Stanley Capital International (MSCI) stock index 28

network theory of contagion 13, 22
Nominal Effective Exchange Rate (NEER) 85

Overnight Index Swap (OIS) 71

Phillips–Perron (PP) test 29, 124
policy coordination 4, 34
principal component analysis 17, 43
private sector 11
public sector 2–3, 5, 11, 22

regime shift (regime switch, regime change) 6, 22, 34, 98, 104, 119, 128
residual bootstrap 123
return spillover 6, 109
risk-free (interest) rate 85, 97
risk management 6, 34, 48, 105, 119
rolling correlation 43

safe-haven currency 45, 49
Schwarz Bayesian information criterion (SBIC) 14, 39, 57, 75, 87
Securities Markets Programme (SMP) 79, 116
sensitivity analysis 4, 41
sovereign CDS 5, 82
spillover index 6, 110
Stability and Growth Pact (SGP) 1
structural break 6, 22, 26, 97, 108, 121
subprime loan 1, 12, 31, 73, 108, 115, 123
systemic failure 13
systemic risk 3, 13, 22

threshold cointegration 6, 122

variance decomposition 109
vector autoregression (VAR) 71, 84
vector error correction model (VECM) 6, 84, 122
volatility persistence 6, 98
volatility spillover 5–6, 37, 58, 72, 108

wake-up call contagion 2
Wald test 84, 124

For Product Safety Concerns and Information please contact our EU
representative GPSR@taylorandfrancis.com Taylor & Francis Verlag GmbH,
Kaufingerstraße 24, 80331 München, Germany

Printed and bound by CPI Group (UK) Ltd, Croydon, CR0 4YY
08/05/2025
01864325-0003